A DICTIONARY OF BUSINESS TERMS

A DICTIONARY OF BUSINESS TERMS

ALEXANDER HAMILTON INSTITUTE

FRANKLIN WATTS
NEW YORK
1987

Library of Congress Cataloging-in-Publication Data

AHI's complete portfolio of modern business terms.
    A dictionary of business terms.

    Previously published as: AHI's complete portfolio of modern business terms. 1986.
        1. Business—Dictionaries.   2. Finance—Dictionaries.
I. Alexander Hamilton Institute (U.S.)   II. Title.
HF1001.A34   1987   650′.03′21   86-24560
ISBN 0-531-15518-8

Copyright © 1986 Alexander Hamilton Institute, Inc.
Printed in the United States of America
All rights reserved
6 5 4 3 2 1

Introduction

The rapid expansion of business in recent years has brought with it a wealth of new words and reinterpretations of old ones. As an executive you must read, think and communicate on all aspects of business terms which transcend your area of business specialty or personal experience.

That's why the Alexander Hamilton Institute developed *A Dictionary of Business Terms*. The editors designed and prepared this up-to-date guide to help you to add clarity and accuracy to all of your business communications—oral and written reports, letters, speeches and presentations.

It gives you immediate access to more than 2,500 business terms covering more than 40 major fields of business activity. You'll find more than 200 terms covering computers and data processing alone. It will speed your report and letter writing and enable you to get your business message across to customers, suppliers, employees and colleagues and avoid costly misunderstandings.

Terms contain multiple definitions whenever they are used in different fields of business with various meanings. And where necessary, you'll find cross references to take you from a specific term to the general term that explains it.

And you'll never again have to waste time poring through standard dictionaries and encyclopedias for a term or definition. You'll be able to put your finger on the right term quickly and easily with the special "business term locator" where every term has been listed again alphabetically in one or more of the following major business areas:

- Data processing
- Financial

- General
- Insurance
- Legal
- Marketing
- Personnel

For example, suppose you want to use the term for protecting your company against employee dishonesty in a letter to an insurance company. You've heard the term, but you can't recall it.

You scan all the terms listed in the "Insurance" category and find the term "fidelity bond." You think that term might be right, but you aren't quite sure. So you look up the term "fidelity bond" in the main listing of terms to find its definition:

> A form of insurance which protects an employer against loss due to the dishonesty of any employee who occupies a position of trust with jurisdiction over funds.

This definition confirms that "fidelity bond" is the term you want, and that your meaning will be crystal-clear.

The editors are confident that you'll keep *A Dictionary of Business Terms* in a prominent place on your desk because you'll refer to it again and again. You'll even want to carry it to meetings and take it with you on business trips.

ABC analysis

An inventory control technique which uses a system of labelling items (A, B, or C) according to their price and turnover frequency.

absenteeism

The failure of workers to report on the job when they are scheduled to work. An employee is considered scheduled to work when the employer has work available, the employee is aware that there is work, and the employer has no reason to suspect in advance that the employee will not be available.

absentee ownership

The ownership of rental property that is located somewhere other than where the owner lives.

absolute advantage

A situation in which a person, business, or nation has an unqualified advantage over parties with whom it trades in producing a given product or performing an economic activity.

accelerated depreciation

> A rapid depreciation allowance taken in accounting either for tax purposes or because of such factors as fast obsolescence of machinery or improper maintenance.

acceleration clause

> A provision in a note or other evidence of debt that, at the option of the holder, the entire unpaid balance becomes due if the debtor defaults in any agreed payments of principal or interest.

acceptance

> An agreement of one to the offer of another by which a contract is formed. The act by which the drawee of a draft or bill of exchange undertakes to pay it according to its terms.

acceptance, bank

> A bank draft or trade acceptance drawn on a bank instead of an individual company. Since a bank's credit is generally better known than that of a business, bank acceptances are often used in international trade.

acceptance, trade

> A time draft or bill of exchange drawn by the seller of merchandise on the buyer for the purchase price of goods. The credit period and place of payment are usually stated on the bill.

access time

> The length of time it takes a computer to locate or use data. A computer locates data in its storage section, and it uses it after transferring the stored memory to the arithmetic unit.

accidental death

In insurance this refers to the death of an insured resulting, directly and independently of all other causes, from bodily injury effected solely through external, violent and accidental means before the 60th anniversary of the insured's birth.

accommodation paper

A note that has been co-signed, usually without consideration, in order to "accommodate" a person with weak credit in obtaining a loan. The accommodation endorser acts as a guarantor or surety.

account

A bookkeeping record of a commercial transaction. A customer or client of a business who buys on time and pays according to some prearranged credit plan.

account, asset

The various things owned by a business enterprise such as cash, stock-in-trade, supplies, machinery, furniture, fixtures and land.

account, capital

The net worth, the capital investment, or the owner's equity. In accounting the term is often used to mean fixed assets as a class.

account, open-book

The seller's accounting record of an unsecured sale of merchandise. A retail charge account.

account, profit and loss

An account opened at the end of a fiscal period for the purpose of collecting the balances of accounts reflecting revenues, incomes, profits, expenses and losses. Its balance - net-income or net-loss - is transferred to earned surplus or some other suitable proprietary account.

account, time deposit

An interest-bearing deposit not subject to withdrawal before a fixed date. The savings deposit of a customer of a bank.

account, zero balance

Zero balance accounts funnel cash quickly into a central or master account which in turn funds all of the satellite accounts. Another type of zero balance account is funded by depositing only the amount of funds needed to clear checks that particular day, thereby maintaining a zero balance at all times.

account executive

Contact person in an advertising or public relations firm who acts as liaison between the agency and client. Officially, he or she represents the agency regarding marketing strategy, copy appeals, art treatment, and over-all management of the account. In investments a person such as an investment advisor who handles clients' accounts.

accountability

Being obligated to stand behind performance. The obligation of a subordinate to report to a superior on the way a delegated job has been performed.

accounting

The science of recording, classifying, verifying, analyzing and interpreting the economic data of an enterprise.

accounting, accrual basis

> A system of accounting which takes cognizance of accrued and deferred revenues and expenses as well as cash revenues and expenses. Also a method of accounting where revenue and expense are identified with a specific period of time such as a month or year as distinguished from cash basis which is defined elsewhere.

accounting, cash basis of

> A system of accounting in which revenue and expense are recorded on the books of account when received or paid, respectively, without regard to the period to which such transactions apply.

accounting, cost

> A form of accounting which is concerned with detailed information about the costs of materials, labor, and overhead, incident to production and distribution of a commodity or to the rendering of a service.

accounting, double entry

> A system of accounting in which an entry in two accounts is made to record each transaction. It is based on the fact that every item of value of whatever kind is owned or claimed by someone. Basic to double entry accounting is the equation: assets are equal to liabilities plus capital.

accounting, payroll

> A type of accounting concerned with information about the payroll of a business enterprise.

accounting, single entry

> A system of accounting which records simply the records of customers, creditors and cash. Each transaction is recorded but once.

accounting department

> The department whose main jobs are keeping an accurate count of the things a business owes and owns and determining the profit or loss of the business.

accounting equation

> The equation, assets = liabilities + capital, upon which double entry accounting is based.

accounting system

> The particular method of accounting adopted by a specific business enterprise.

accounts, uncollectible and execution proof

> Accounts receivable which defy all efforts to collect, and which the debtors, because they own no property, cannot be forced to pay even though there is resort to legal action.

accounts payable

> Amounts owed to another business because of credit purchases. The records showing persons from whom purchases were made on account and the status of the liability accounts.

accounts receivable

> Unsecured assets due a business arising from all credit sales. The records showing persons or businesses to whom merchandise was sold on account and the status of the accounts.

accreditation

> The recognition of an organization or program as meeting certain standards as prescribed by an authorized or respected body or agency.

accrued expense

    An account on an income statement indicating an obligation which has been contracted but not yet paid.

accrued income

    An account on an income statement indicating earnings which have not yet been received.

accumulated depreciation

    Also called accrued depreciation. Refers to the total amount of an asset's value that has been decreased due to usage, passage of time, wear and tear, etc.

accumulator

    A term used in connection with computers meaning a device which stores the results of mathematical operations.

acid test

    The same as acid test ratio. See ratio, acid test.

acoustic coupler

    A device that enables access between a computer terminal and a CPU, usually via a standard telephone line.

acquisition

    The takeover of one company by another. See also merger.

across-the-board

> An expression that means to include everyone or everything, such as an across-the-board increase in taxes or an across-the-board decrease in wages.

act of God

> A cause of injury or damage that human ability cannot reasonably avoid or foresee such as an earthquake or a tornado.

actuary

> A person who calculates insurance probabilities and determines premiums based on estimates of interest earnings, mortality rates, and the like.

address code

> In computer language, this term refers to a letter or number or both which indicate where a specific piece of information can be found in the storage unit of the computer.

ad hoc committee

> Ad hoc literally means "for this." Such a committee is organized for a specific purpose and is disbanded when the job is completed.

adjustable rate mortgage (ARM)

> A mortgage which has variable terms, such as payment or interest rate terms, that are adjusted periodically during the life of the mortgage contract. This is distinguished from a fixed rate mortgage which is defined elsewhere.

adjusting entries

    Bookkeeping accounts which follow the preparation of the trial balance and precede the closing entries. Their purpose is to make the adjustments to income and expense accounts necessary for accounting on an accrual basis.

adjustment

    An entry or entries to correct or modify accounts, especially entries at the end of an accounting period. Also, a cash or credit allowance made on merchandise which did not prove satisfactory to the buyer.

adjustment letter

    A letter sent by a business making an adjustment to a customer who was not satisfied with a transaction.

adjustor

    A person who investigates insurance damage caused by fire or other disaster and who attempts to arrive at a satisfactory settlement with the insured.

administration

    The planning, organizing, coordinating, directing, and controlling of a business toward its stated objectives.

administrative assistant

    An employee who handles some administrative functions as well as the routine clerical duties of a secretary.

administrative law

> That area of law which governs the actions and procedures of administrative agencies (i.e. organizations given power by a federal, state or municipal government to act as their agent).

administrator

> A person who manages business affairs of any kind. A person authorized to settle an estate when the deceased has left no will or has named no executor.

ad valorem duty

> A customs tax placed on the value of imported goods.

advance

> The amount of principal in a credit transaction. Also, the furnishing of something on contract before the value for it is received, such as a salary advance for a salesperson given in anticipation of earnings.

advance card

> A card designed as an aid to a salesperson, used to announce to a buyer that a salesperson will call at a certain time.

advance commitment

> In selling a bond issue, this refers to the agreement by a private buyer to take up the issue at a future date.

advance press

> In order to promote or publicize a new product, event, or start-up, a public relations drive is initiated in order to alert the media that a new product is about to be launched. Such advance press, or notice, allows the members of the media to be aware of the new product and to follow up with relevant queries and related news stories and articles.

advertising

> Any form of paid announcement intended to aid directly or indirectly in the sales of a commodity or service. The act or business of preparing or circulating advertisements.

advertising, black and white

> A space advertisement that appears with black print on white paper as distinguished from an advertisement which employs colors.

advertising, color

> Any paid form of advertising which uses color as an integral part of the presentation.

advertising, commodity

> That form of advertising which is designed to point up the virtues of or call attention to a specific commodity or group of commodities.

advertising, cooperative

> When advertising is paid for jointly by the retailer and the manufacturer.

advertising, direct mail

> Any kind of advertising that goes directly to the prospective buyer through the mail, including letters, booklets, samples, folders and leaflets.

advertising, institutional

> Advertising which seeks to build good will with the public or with business organiztions and does not expect direct action.

advertising, point of purchase

Advertising designed to attract the consumer public in retail stores at the place where the product is bought.

advertising, public relations

Advertising such as institutional advertising designed to gain the good will of the public, such as stockholders, suppliers, employees and consumers.

advertising, remembrance

Advertising placed in media of a long-lasting nature, such as calendars, novelties, playing cards and leather goods, designed to serve as a reminder to selected audiences of the name, the products and the address of a business firm.

advertising, word of mouth

The process by which individual customers of a product or service communicate the value or worth of that product or service to one's associates, friends, family, and so on. This "word of mouth" advertising can be either of a positive or negative nature.

advertising agency

An organization which prepares and places advertisements for clients, helps in sales promotion material, and often advises on overall marketing problems.

advertising allowance

The portion of cost the manufacturer bears toward the promotion and advertising of his product at the wholesale or retail level. The amount of advertising expense for which a wholesaler or retailer is reimbursed by the manufacturer.

advertising campaign

> A series of advertisements, using a definite theme or appeal, planned to accomplish a specific task.

advertising folder

> A pamphlet, brochure or folded paper on which a printed advertisement appears.

advertising manager

> The person who plans advertising policies and arranges for the execution of these policies. The person in charge of advertising for a business firm.

advertising media

> Avenues through which advertising and public relations messages are transmitted to the public, such as newspapers, magazines, radio, television, direct mail, billboards and posters.

advertising promotion

> The area of advertising concerned with the mechanical steps necessary for the preparation of advertisements.

advertising specialty

> A low cost item, imprinted with a company logo or message, distributed to potential buyers of the company's goods or services.

affidavit

> A written statement or testimony made before a notary public or other person authorized by law to administer an oath or affirmation.

affirmative action

> The requirement that firms or other organizations take positive actions to remedy the imbalance of past employment practices that may have discriminated against hiring members of minority groups.

after-acquired clause

> A written stipulation in a mortgage bond which provides that any property acquired after the contract will be subject to the mortgage.

aftermarket sales

> The sale of additional or updated equipment to accompany a previously purchased product.

agate line

> A printing and typesetting term used to describe the smallest size letters found in most magazines and newspapers. Commonly used with legal notices in newspapers.

age certification

> Also called working papers. Documentation proving that a minor is of legal working age.

aged receivables report

> See aging schedule.

agency

> A business relationship between two parties whereby one party, the principal, delegates certain powers of acting in his or her behalf to the other party, the agent.

agent

>A person who acts on behalf of another person, his principal, in conducting transactions with a third person.

agent, export

>A middleman who represents foreign buyers in a market.

agent, import

>A middleman who represents foreign sellers in a market.

aging schedule

>A financial management report showing outstanding invoices and the amount of time they have been unpaid. Frequently, the period of time is stated as over 30 days; over 60 days; over 90 days or longer.

agio

>A premium paid to exchange one currency for another.

air express

>The shipment of goods by air, a service which is provided by the Railway Express Agency. Up to a certain weight, this form of transportation is less expensive than air freight.

air freight

>The shipment of goods by air, a service which is provided by the airlines. Beyond a certain weight, this form of transportation becomes less expensive than air express.

ALGOL

Acronym for algorithmic language. A programming language used on minicomputers and mainframes, adapted to mathematical and logical problems.

allonge

A separate sheet of paper attached to a negotiable instrument to provide space for additional endorsements.

allowance

A credit in lieu of a cash refund given to a customer who is not satisfied with a business transaction.

all-savers certificate

Certificates of deposit offered by thrift institutions with the terms that the first $1000.00 of interest earned was exempt from federal income tax.

alpha-numeric card code

A form of punched card which is used to communicate with a computer. The card employs both the alphabet and numbers. The alphabetic characters are represented by two punches in a vertical column; the numbers zero through nine are coded as a single punch in a vertical column.

ALU

Abbreviation for arithmetic logic unit. The part of a microprocessor that performs mathematical and logical problems.

amalgamation

    The process of forming an entirely new company by combining two or more exisitng companies.

amicus curiae

    Literally means "friend of the court." Refers to a person who is allowed to participate in court in a law suit on behalf of one side or the other without being called in any of the usual ways (i.e. as a witness for the defense or the prosecution).

amortization

    A method of systematically liquidating a debt. The write-off of intangible assets as opposed to the depreciation of tangible assets.

analog computer

    A computer which accepts information in the form of quantities rather than numbers and which continuously offers the solution to the problem it is solving.

annual earnings

    The total amount of wages received in a year, including base pay, overtime, bonuses and the like.

annuitant

    A person insured under an annuity plan.

annuity

    A form of insurance which, in return for an agreed-on premium, provides the insured or annuitant a regular income immediately or after he reaches a specified age.

annuity, group

> A pension plan which provides for annuities at retirement for a group of persons covered under a master contract, issued to an employer for the benefit of his employees.

annuity, joint survivorship

> A form of annuity which provides income payments until the joint heirs, such as a husband and wife, have both died.

antitrust

> A term used to describe any policies or actions designed to limit or curtail monopoly power.

APL

> Abbreviation for a programming language. Written for minicomputers and mainframes, this high level language is used for complex interactive programming.

appeal

> In law, this refers to a request for a higher court to review a decision handed down by a lower court. In marketing, an appeal is the point of view of an advertisement as it relates to a targeted market.

appellant

> One who appeals a court case.

apple polisher

> A derogatory expression used to describe a person who will do anything to get into the good graces of his or her supervisor or other superiors.

applicant

>Someone who applies or makes a request for something, such as a person applying for a position with a business firm.

application

>A form used in submitting a request for something, such as an application for a job. Also, a given type of job to be done with a computer. Accounts receivable, inventory control and word processing are typical applications.

application software

>A computer program written for a specific application.

appraisal

>An evaluation of property such as real estate, made by a person authorized to do so.

appraisal, performance

>A periodic objective evaluation of an employee's work effort conducted by the employee's supervisor using objective measures or criteria. A performance appraisal usually accompanies one's salary increment.

apprenticeship

>The learning of an art, trade or calling by practical experience, under the guidance and instruction of skilled workers.

arbitrage

>The act of buying such things as commodities, securities or bills of exchange in one market and simultaneously selling in another market where the price is higher.

arbitrager

>A person who buys and sells simultaneously in two markets in order to make a profit.

arbitration

>The act of hearing and determining the cause in controversy between parties by a person or persons who are either chosen by the parties involved or are appointed.

arbitration, compulsory

>The forcing of both parties to a labor-management dispute, upon failure to settle their differences by other means, to refer their respective positions to a third party who acts as judge and whose final decision is binding on both sides.

arbitration, voluntary

>The free decision on the part of both parties in a labor-managment dispute to refer their respective positions to a third party who acts as judge. In such a case, the decision of the arbiter becomes morally binding on both sides.

arithmetic average

>The kind of average computed by totaling the measurements and dividing by the number of cases.

arithmetic unit

>That part of a computer where the functions of adding, subtracting, multiplying, dividing and comparing are performed.

arrangement

In English law an agreement between a debtor and his creditors, modifying his obligations to them in order that he may work out his difficulties to the mutual benefit of himself and them. A U.S. Congressional act of 1938 providing that a debtor may file an "arrangement" either in a pending bankruptcy proceeding or where no proceeding has yet been started.

array

In a computer program, this term refers to a gathering of data in an ordered group, most often in columns and rows. On an electronic component, an array is a group of individual circuits or transistors. In statistics, this term is used to signify an orderly arrangement of all data to be used in a computation.

arrears

An obligation which remains unpaid beyond the date of maturity.

articles of incorporation

The same as certificate of incorporation. See definition of certificate of incorporation.

articles of partnership

A written agreement between partners in a business, outlining the provisions of their business arrangement.

artificial intelligence

The field of study whose practical goal is to make computers mimic human thought and language, or at least give the appearance of doing so, to make them easier to use.

ASCII

>Acronym for American standard code for information interchange. The most widely used code for converting text and numbers to a format suitable for computers to interpret.

asked

>In investments this term refers to the lowest price a seller will take for a security at any given time.

assembler

>A specialized computer program which takes a program written in a language such as ALGOL, APL or BASIC, and converts it into the machine language which the computer uses internally.

assembling

>The act of making one unit out of parts which are in themselves finished products.

assembly language

>A programming language very close to that used by a specific computer internally; varies among computers; difficult to learn and time-consuming to write, but runs most efficiently.

assertiveness training

>A program designed to increase the performance of managers and employees alike by teaching them to respond to situations in a manner that is neither passive nor aggressive but somewhere in between.

assessment

> The charging of property owners for an improvement which is presumed to be a direct benefit to those so charged. Assessment insurance refers to a type of organization which charges each member of the group, in lieu of a premium paid in advance, a fixed sum equal to the losses incurred.

asset

> Something of value that is owned.

assets, current

> Cash and other assets readily converted into cash, such as accounts receivable, inventory and some prepaid expenses.

assets, fixed

> A term used in a balance sheet to denote assets of a lasting nature that can be used repeatedly such as a building or machinery and that are not readily convertible into cash.

assets, frozen

> Assets which cannot be converted into cash in the foreseeable future.

assets, intangible

> Assets such as goodwill, patents and organization costs, grouped under the caption "intangibles" in a model balance sheet.

assign

> To transfer property, a right, or an interest, especially in trust.

assigned risk

> In insurance, this terms refers to that group of risks which insurance companies do not wish to underwrite, but which by law must be insured. The risks are assigned from a general pool to individual insurance companies.

assignee

> A person, often a creditor, to whom property, a right, or an interest is transferred.

assignment

> An instrument of transfer. A transference of property, right, interest or title.

assignment, absolute

> In insurance this term referes to the turning over of title, right, and interests of an assignor to an assignee.

assignment, collateral

> In insurance this term refers to the turning over the rights of an insurance policy to protect a creditor. The pledging of the cash values of a policy as collateral for a loan.

assignment of wages

> A transfer of a portion of one's wages to another by direct payment from the employer. This agreement is directed by the employee, as distinguished from garnishment, a court-ordered payment of wages, which is defined elsewhere.

assumed obligation

>The agreement, usually for a consideration, by one person or company to pay the principal and interest or the interest but not the principal of a loan made to another person or company.

assumption of a debt

>An agreement to pay the debt of another.

asynchronous communication

>A format for exchanging data between computers. Data are sent along with information that signals the beginning and end of each transmission. Not as fast as some other types of communication. See also synchronous communication.

attachment

>A writ by which a sheriff is ordered to seize certain property of a defendant so as to secure the plaintiff in collecting his claim.

attrition

>In cost control this refers to the diminishing of value of industrial inventories through loss, spoilage, clerical error, petty theft, unreported scrap, padded production costs, and similar influences.

audience

>In advertising this refers to the readers, listeners, or viewers of an advertising message.

audimeter

>Also known as the Nielsen survey. A mechanical instrument used in audience research which makes a minute-by-minute graphic record of radio or television audience habits.

audit

> An official or regular examination and verification of financial accounts and records of a business firm.

auditing

> The systematic examination of records and documents to determine the legality of transactions and the accuracy of records.

auditing department

> That part of a business organization in which the work of auditors is performed.

auditor

> A person who examines accounts through a systematic method in order to determine the legality of transactions and the accuracy of records.

authorized

> The amount of various classes of stock permitted to be issued by a company's charter. Also, the amount of bonds, secured by one mortgage, which can be issued; or the amount of bonds, authorized for each series, which can be issued.

automatic premium loan

> A provision in a life insurance contract that can be selected by the insured to keep the policy in force. It provides that if any premium is due and unpaid, the company can deduct that premium from the cash value of the policy.

automation

The use of methods, machinery, tools and facilities to maximize productive efficiency.

auxiliary storage

Also called secondary storage. An additional storage unit that supplements the computer's primary storage. Such "backup" units are usually in the form of a disk or magnetic tape.

average

In statistics, the measurement of central tendency is called the average. There are three kinds of averages: the arithmetic average, the median and the mode. These three averages are defined elsewhere.

average, moving

A statistical method of smoothing out fluctuation of data in a trend by dropping out the oldest item and including the newest item in the series in the calculation of each successive average.

averages

In investments this term refers to calculations which give the mean price of selected securities. A series of such calculations reflect the general trend of the market.

averaging down

The act of purchasing securities at a lower price than that paid for securities already owned in order to reduce the average cost per unit. For example, 100 shares bought at $80 followed by 100 shares bought at $70 average $75 per share for the 200 shares owned.

B

back order

> A request for goods that cannot be immediately filled due to lack of inventory. Such an order is filled when the goods come in, without the customer having to reorder.

back pay

> Payment of wages that have been delayed for a period of time.

backlog

> A reserve or accumulation of unfilled orders.

backup

> Any planned and executed process that provides for the saving and security of information in the event of computer failure. It may be regular saving of data into separate storage, or off-site physical storage, duplicate processors, etc.

bad debt

> A debt which is uncollectible.

bailee

> A person who receives goods or property from another person under contract of bailment.

bailment

> The act of an owner of goods turning them over to another for repair, storage, rental, safekeeping, or the like.

bailment, gratuitous

> A bailment which does not involve a return, compensation, or consideration.

bailment, storage

> The act of placing or storing goods under the responsibility of a bailee in a warehouse or other depository.

bailment, warehouse

> The act of placing or storing goods, whose title has not yet been transferred, in a warehouse under the reponsibility of a bailee.

Bakke decision

> A landmark reverse discrimination case where the court found that Allan Bakke had been discriminated against by the University of California Medical School at Davis in favor of minority applicants. See also reverse discrimination.

balance of stores ledger

> A ledger form used by the purchasing department to keep a record of materials on hand, on order, available, and apportioned against planned orders.

balance of trade

> A situation which exists in foreign trade when a nation's exports equal its imports in a given period. The expression can be used to refer to the nation's total exports and imports or to its exports and imports as related to each nation with which it trades.

balance of trade, favorable

> A situation which exists in foreign trade when a nation's exports exceed its imports.

balance of trade, unfavorable

> A situation which exists in foreign trade when a nation's imports exceed its exports.

balance sheet

> A statement which reports the financial condition of a business as of a specific date, usually at the end of a fiscal period. A statement listing the assets, liabilities and capital structure of an organization as of a specific date.

balance sheet equation

> The equation that assets equal liabilities plus net worth, which serves as the basis for double entry accounting.

balloon maturity

> A large final payment of a term loan following a series of lesser payments.

ballpark figure

> A rough estimate.

band printer

    A type of impact printer which prints a line of characters at a time via a stainless steel band imprinted with all possible characters. A very common type of line printer.

bandwidth

    The frequency of a specific component—microprocessor, cable or video monitor. The bandwidth expresses how much electrical activity the component can perform in a second and determines its speed and how much data it can handle.

bank

    An establishment designed primarily to receive deposits and to loan money.

bank, commercial

    An institution engaged primarily in the receiving of demand deposits, more familiarly known as checking accounts, and in the making of short-term loans.

bank, correspondent

    A bank which carries on continuing, mutually advantageous business and financial relations with a bank in some other locality.

bank, investment

    A security house. A bank which sells issues of bonds, preferred stocks, and common stocks of old and new companies.

bank, national

    A commercial bank which is chartered by the federal government rather than by the state in which it operates.

bank, savings

An institution engaged primarily in receiving time deposits, more familiarly known as savings accounts, and in making relatively long-term extensions of credit.

bank, state

A commercial bank which is chartered by the state in which it operates rather than by the federal government.

bank, wildcat

A bank which, in order to avoid honoring its circulating notes, was organized in a sparsely settled area where reputedly there were more wildcats than people.

bank acceptance

A method of making payment for merchandise through the use of the purchaser's bank. The instrument or draft is drawn on and accepted by the purchaser's bank through prior arrangements made between the seller, purchaser, and the purchaser's bank.

bank balance

The difference between the amount of money deposited to an account in a bank and the amount withdrawn.

bank charge

The fees a bank collects from its customers for certain services, such as a bank charge for maintenance of checking accounts, for stop payment orders, for issuing money orders, and the like.

bank credit

> Credit created by a bank by depositing the proceeds of a loan to the borrower's account.

bank deposits

> Money placed or entrusted to a bank for safekeeping or for earning interest. There are two well-known kinds of bank deposits: demand deposits and time deposits.

bank holiday

> A legal holiday when banks, as well as most businesses, are closed. In the U.S. such holidays include Christmas Day, New Year's Day, Thanksgiving Day, Independence Day, Labor Day and Memorial Day.

bank money

> An order to a bank to transfer deposit credits on the books of the bank. Such bank money served as money in the 17th century in Amsterdam.

bank statement

> A statement sent out monthly by a bank to depositors listing the checks drawn, the daily deposits, service charges and the daily balance of an account.

bankruptcy

> The state of a person who is legally declared unable to pay his or her debts.

bankruptcy, involuntary

> The condition of a debtor who has been adjudged insolvent and whose property is turned over to a trustee for the benefit of creditors. In involuntary bankruptcy, the petition is filed by the creditors.

bankruptcy, voluntary

> An act by which a business or an individual declares of his own volition that the money that he owes exceeds the assets he owns and that he be adjudged bankrupt.

bar code reader

> An optical scanning device, used frequently in grocery stores to read bar codes (such as a universal product code) imprinted on items and merchandise.

bargain counter

> The purchase of securities at price lower than their apparent value in a market. Also, a counter in a retail store where merchadise is sold at bargain prices.

bargaining

> A procedure in reaching an agreement between parties, such as labor and management settling what each shall give and receive.

bargaining, collective

> See definition of collective bargaining.

bargaining, individual

> A situation in which each worker individually bargains with management as distinguished from collective bargaining.

barometers

    Statistical data compiled in such a way that it forecasts future trends of business activity and of market price action.

barter

    The direct exchange of one commodity for another without the use of money or of a medium of exchange.

base pay

    A wage exclusive of overtime, bonus, or premium of any kind.

base year analysis

    A method of analyzing financial statements over a series of years by comparing figures for each of the years with those of a common base year.

BASIC

    Acronym for beginners' all-purpose symbolic instruction code. The most popular language for microcomputers developed in the late 1940's at Dartmouth College. A high level programming language that is relatively easy to learn and use.

basing point price system

    A method, leading to broader market distribution, by which business firms quote prices based on a common location, regardless of where production actually takes place. Buyers are often forced to pay "phantom" freight charges and producers can shift the basing point to meet or beat local competitors.

batch processing

> The processing of data in groups at fixed intervals as distinguished from immediate processing. See also immediate processing.

bath

> Also big bath, taking a bath, or bloodbath. All are slang expressions referring to a great, unexpected monetary loss.

baud

> The transmission speed of a device, equal to the number of bits per second.

bear

> In investments and speculation, this term refers to a person who is pessimistic about the level of stock prices and believes they will decline.

bear market

> A market in which the primary trend or direction of security or commodity prices is downward, with successive rallies falling short of previous highs and successive low points falling below previous lows.

bearer

> A person who holds a check, note, or other such instrument which in due course can be collected from the drawer.

behavior modification

> A term used in management to refer to a method of training personnel by use of positive and negative reinforcement as reward or punishment for specific kinds of behavior.

benchmark jobs

> Key jobs in job evaluation. Those jobs which differ sufficiently one from another so that they can be distinguished, but at the same time they represent the various levels of the whole scale, ranging from the lowest to the highest valued positions to be rated.

beneficiary

> A person named to receive the legacy of a will or the proceeds of an insurance policy. The person designated to receive the income of a trust estate.

benefit period

> The period of time specified by law or contract in which an employee may qualify for payments under an insurance policy.

bequest

> Also known as a legacy. A gift of personal property given by one person to another in a will.

beta coefficient

> A measurement describing the movement of a particular stock as it relates to the movement of the stock market as a whole.

Better Business Bureau

> An agency, organized for the protection of consumers, which operates by exposing unethical or delinquent business practices on the part of firms and other organizations.

bid

> The price offered by those wishing to buy given stocks or bonds. Also, the price the dealer will pay for securities of the investor. Also, the prices offered in competitive bidding by financial houses competing for a new security issue. Also, a competitive offer in order to get a contract to do work.

Big Board

> A term meaning the New York Stock Exchange.

Big Eight

> This term refers to the eight largest public accounting firms, including Arthur Andersen and Co.; Coopers and Lybrand; Ernst and Ernst; Haskins and Sells; Peat, Marwick, Mitchell and Co.; Price Waterhouse and Co.; Touche Ross and Co.; and Arthur Young and Co.

Big Three

> This term refers to the three largest automobile manufacturers in the U.S., General Motors Corp., Ford Motor Co., and Chrysler Corp.

bilateral contract

> A contract formed by a promise given by one party in exchange for a promise from another party.

billing

> The act of sending a bill or a notice to pay to a person or firm owing money. The procedure of sending a statement of what is due and payable by a business firm who sold or delivered goods or services under some agreed upon credit arrangement.

billing, cycle

> A system of billing whereby a company will mail out a certain number of statements each day or at periodic intervals during the month in order to balance the workload for this kind of work.

bill of exchange

> A draft used in foreign exchange. A written order addressed by one person (the drawer) to another person (the drawee) directing the person to whom it is addressed to pay a specified sum of money on demand or at a fixed or determinable future time. The term is often used interchangeably with draft or acceptance.

bill of lading

> A document issued by a common carrier to a shipper acknowledging the receipt of goods and agreeing to transport them under the conditions stipulated.

bill of lading, negotiable

> A form of bill of lading which states that goods described therein will be delivered to bearer or to someone named in the document. Such a bill of lading is negotiable and can circulate as money.

bill of lading, non-negotiable

> A form of bill of lading which provides that the goods described therein will be delivered only to the consignee.

bill of lading, order

> A form of bill of lading which states that goods are consigned "to the order of" any person named in such a bill.

bill of lading, straight

A form of bill of lading which states that goods are consigned to a specific person without any "order" words appearing in the contract.

bill of material

A written form used in production control which consists of a list of the finished parts, subassemblies, and assemblies which are needed to fill an order.

bill of sale

A written statement certifying that the ownership of something has been transferred by sale.

bill of sale, conditional

A written statement certifying that the ownership of something which has been sold will be transferred upon compliance with specified conditions.

bimodal distribution

A frequency distribution which has two modes, or two groups of frequently occurring numbers. This would be represented on a graph by two peaks.

binary card code

A form of punched card which is used to communicate with a computer. The card is made up of combinations of two characters, zero and one. Information is communicated only by the presence or absence of a punch—the presence of a punch indicating a one and the absence a zero.

binary coded decimal

    An expresion used in computer language referring to a system of representing each decimal digit by a combination of four digits. For example, the binary code of 0000 equals the decimal code for "0," the binary code of 0001 equals the decimal code for "1."

binary digit

    Also called a bit. A unit of a number in the binary numbering system. For example, since there are just two possible numbers in the system, "zero" and "one," a combination of these numbers might be 100101. There are six units or digits in this number.

binary input

    An expression which refers to the process by which an operator communicates information to a digital computer by means of the binary number system. In the binary number system there are two numbers: zero and one.

binder

    In insurance this term refers to a temporary document or oral commitment by an agent certifying that a risk is covered. An insurance policy usually replaces the binder within a limited period of time. In real estate a binder is a receipt for a sum of money which has been made to secure the right to purchase a property upon agreed terms.

bit

    Contraction of binary digit. The smallest unit of data which a computer understands. Represented by 0 to 1.

black box

> A term referring to a concept that unknown processes take place between inputs and results.

black market

> A term used to refer to the buying or selling of scarce products and commodities, including currencies, in violation of government regulations.

blackleg

> See definition of scab.

blanket agreement

> A collective bargaining agreement that is based on industrywide negotiations that cover a large geographic area within an industry.

blanket order

> An order for a large quantity of goods to be delivered over a period of time, usually a year.

blanket policy

> A broad insurance policy covering a variety of items that would otherwise be insured separately. Used commonly in fire and burglary insurance where an entire property and its contents are insured by a single policy.

blind advertisement

> An advertisement which does not have a company name or signature on it. A common example is a help-wanted advertisement in the classified section of a newspaper, describing the position but not naming the company involved.

blind pair comparison

    Testing a product's appeal to consumers by having them compare it with another similar product, not knowing which is which, and recording the results.

block style

    A form of business letter in which there is no indentation made for the opening line of a paragraph.

blue collar workers

    Those workers engaged in physical labor, usually production and maintenance work in factories, construction sites, and farming. Blue collar workers are distinguished from white and grey collar workers, both of which are defined elsewhere.

blue laws

    State or local legislation that restricts business activities on Sundays.

blue sky law

    A name given to laws enacted by various states regulating the sale and issuance of securities in order to prevent fraud.

board of directors

    A body of people, elected by stockholders, who direct the affairs and establish the policies of a corporation.

boiler room operation

    A term used in investments to refer to a brokerage firm which sells stocks of questionable value by telephone.

bond

> A written obligation under seal. A certificate of indebtedness based upon the sale of a bond. A form of long-term indebtedness.

bond, accumulation

> A bond such as the "E" series U.S. government bond which is sold at a discount and, if held, full interest is realized when the bond matures. This differs from annual or semiannual interest on a principal amount invested.

bond, assumed

> A bond on which a corporation other than the issuer has undertaken to pay interest and principal as they fall due.

bond, baby

> A bond whose denomination or face value is $500 or less.

bond, bail

> A bond guaranteeing the appearance of a prisoner before the court at the time of his trial or whenever required.

bond, bankers' and brokers' blanket

> A fidelity bond which provides protection against losses incurred by financial institutions.

bond, bearer

> A type of bond whose face amount is payable to the holder. The owner's name is not registered.

bond, blanket position

    A fidelity bond which protects a company from liability due to the dishonesty of any employee of the firm.

bond, collateral trust

    A bond secured by personal property which is deposited with a trust company to be held for the benefit of the bondholder in the event of default.

bond, continued

    A bond that cannot be called prior to its maturity date. Also called a non-callable bond.

bond, contract

    A bond which assumes the liability for the principal's failure to perform a designated task, such as the construction of a building.

bond, convertible

    A bond giving the holder the right to exchange it for some other type of security, usually common or preferred stock.

bond, cost

    A bond guaranteeing the payment of costs in any action at law.

bond, coupon

    A bond which has coupons attached to it for each date on which interest is due. The corporation does not keep a record of the owner of such a bond. Interest is paid to the party who presents the dated coupons.

bond, debenture

> An unsecured bond backed only by the credit standing of the issuing agency.

bond, divisional

> A bond secured by a lien on a branch or division of a railroad and not upon the mail line or the entire mileage.

bond, equipment trust

> A bond used to finance the purchase of railroad rolling stock and other equipment. Title to the equipment is held by a trustee who issues the bonds, pledging it as security. The bond is an obligation of the company purchasing the equipment.

bond, fidelity

> A form of insurance which protects an employer against loss due to the dishonesty of any employee who occupies a position of trust with jurisdiction over funds.

bond, fiduciary

> A bond offering protection to an estate by guaranteeing that the estate entrusted to a fiduciary will not be lessened due to dishonesty or negligence of the fiduciary.

bond, forgery and alteration

> A fidelity bond which provides protection against loss caused by the forgery or alteration of commercial instruments.

bond, guaranteed

> A bond on which payments are guarantees by another corporation.

bond, income

    A bond which provides that the payment of interest is based upon current earnings, and no interest need be paid on it if there is no income from which to pay it.

bond, license and permit

    A bond required by many governmental bodies of such persons as pawnbrokers, plumbers, electricians, and the like, as a guarantee of proper compliance with statutory requirements and municipal ordinances.

bond, lost-instrument

    A bond which undertakes to indemnify the issuer of a document of consequences that may arise from possession of the document by others than the recognized owner.

bond, mortgage

    A bond which pledges real estate as security. Such a bond is usually classified as first, second, or third, depending on the priority of its claims against the security.

bond, names-schedule

    A fidelity bond which covers several employees of a firm by listing their names on a schedule attached to the bond.

bond, petitioning or creditors'

    A bond providing that if a petition in bankruptcy filed by creditors against a debtor is dismissed, the bonding company will pay to the debtor all expenses, costs, and damages.

bond, position-schedule

A fidelity bond which covers any employee of a business firm who occupies the position named in the schedule attached to the bond.

bond, premium

A bond which is sold for more than its face value.

bond, profit sharing

A bond which not only receives a guaranteed interest rate but also participates in the profits of the company issuing it.

bond, public-official

A fidelity bond which provides coverage against loss due to dishonesty or mishandling of public funds by a public official.

bond, refunding

A bond that is used to retire other indebtednesss.

bond, registered

A kind of bond the name of whose holder is kept by the corporation and interest for which is mailed to the holder when due.

bond, revenue

A bond sold to obtain money for the purpose of building a facility, the use of which will require tolls or rents to be paid. These tolls are to produce the revenue to meet the obligations contracted by sale of the bond.

bond, serial

> A bond issue which matures in installments over a period of years. Such bonds are widely used in state and municipal bond-financing where regular tax revenues can be counted on to repay them.

bond, sheriff indemnity

> A bond providing that a sheriff undertaking a seizure of goods will be reimbursed if he or she is held liable in damages in an action brought against him for unlawful seizure.

bond, sinking fund

> A bond issue which provides that the issuing company will deposit annually with a trustee an amount of money that will equal the amount due by the time the bond expires.

bond averages

> Calculations which give the mean price of selected bonds. A series of such calculations reflect the general trend of the bond market.

bond discount

> The amount by which a bond sells below its face value when it is purchased.

bond yields

> The return to a bond investor based on what he paid. This consists of interest plus the increase in principal if the bond is bought below call price. The yield is usually expressed as a percentage figure.

bond yield to maturity

> The calculation of the precise return a bond will pay when it matures at par, based on the price paid for it at the time it was purchased.

bonus

> A payment which is in addition to payments normally due for services rendered. A method of compensation over and above base salary or wages.

bonus, attendance

> A periodic award or bonus paid employees for perfect attendance in the form of fixed cash sums or in the nature of extra time off, such as additional vacation days.

bonus, cost of living

> A bonus geared to the cost of living index in recognition of the fact that higher costs of living without an increase in money wages result in a reduction in the amount of real wages.

bonus, merit

> A payment, in addition to what is usually due, given because of meritorious or praiseworthy service.

bonus, recruitment

> A bonus paid employees for efforts they expend in helping recruit new employees.

bonus, stock

> A bonus paid employees in the form of company stock.

book value

> The value of anything as ascertained by the books of account of the person or business owning it. The net amount at which an asset or asset group appears on the books of account. The quotient of the assets less the liabilities divided by the number of shares outstanding.

bookkeeper

> A person who keeps business records of sales, output, costs and expenses. A person who performs the routine functions of accounting for a business firm.

boom

> A period of prosperity characterized by expansion of business activity and by rapid rise in market values.

boot

> A payment or an amount given in addition to an exchange of things in order to equalize the exchange or trade. For example, when two real estate properties of unequal values are traded, a boot makes up the difference in value. Also, the process of turning on a computer, or a program, and getting it up and running.

bootstrap program

> The program that automatically boots up a microcomputer when it is turned on. The program is part of the computer itself. See also firmware.

borrower

> The recipient of a loan.

bottleneck inflation

> A rise in the general price level or in the prices of certain goods, due to a sudden reduction in supply or sudden increase in demand. The resulting interruption of the flow of normal operations is called a "bottleneck."

bottom line

> A term meaning the final conclusion or result, such as the final profit or loss figure for an accounting period.

bourse

> A place developed in the 16th and 17th centuries, first in Antwerp, then in London and elsewhere, where loanable capital was collected and disbursed without the use of actual gold or silver. The term used in France for a stock exchange.

boycott

> The act of union members of refraining from purchasing products of companies whose employees are on strike or of companies who are in conflict with a union.

boycott, primary

> A situation where union members refuse to purchase the products of a company.

boycott, secondary

> A boycott in which workers refuse to purchase products from suppliers of a non-union plant or of a plant where a strike is going on.

bpi

> Abbreviation for bits per inch. A measurement of computer tape density. For example, a density of 500 bpi indicates capacity of 500 characters per inch.

brainstorming

> A group effort aimed at generating creative ideas for new products, problem solving, or other business-related activities.

branch

> A subordinate local office which is part of a central system, such as the branch office of a national business organization.

branch manager

> A person responsible for the activities of a subordinate office which is part of a central system.

branching

> A term in computer language which refers to the way the next operation is chosen while a program is in progress, adding greatly to the flexibility of a machine.

brand

> A name, term, symbol, or design, or a combination of them, which identifies and distiguishes the goods and services of a seller.

brand, national

> The name of a product which is sold throughout the country as distinguished from a private brand which is defined elsewhere.

brassage

    A charge, not exceeding the actual cost of coinage, levied for coining bullion. Compare with seigniorage, which is defined elsewhere.

breach of contract

    Failure to fulfill contractual responsibilities, often resulting in legal action being taken against the party who broke the agreement.

breach of promise

    The failure to perform a duty which has been agreed upon by contract.

break-even analysis

    A financial tool for determining the point in sales where the total costs are equal to total revenues. Break-even analysis shows how many sales are needed to break even or earn a specific amount of profit.

break-even chart

    A chart used in budgetary control on which the break-even point is shown and which presents relationships between volume, costs, prices and profits.

broadside

    An advertisement or piece of promotion consisting of a single large sheet of paper, usually printed on only one side. A jumbo or monarch size folder which opens to a single display, divided into neither pages nor columns.

broker

An agent who represents either buyer or seller. He seldom has physical access to the goods with which he deals, and has limited powers as to prices and terms of sale. The term broker is often applied to institutions and individuals active in the investment field. One who acts for sellers or buyers of stocks and bonds. The term also is used in insurance, real estate and personnel placement.

brokerage

The fee or commission received for transacting business as a broker.

brokerage house

A business which is engaged in the buying and selling of stocks and bonds.

bucket shop

A term used in investments to refer to an illegal operation where the broker may not execute a client's order to buy or sell. In effect, the broker gambles that the market will go in a different direction than that expected by the client.

budget

A target, in so far as plans, income and expenditures are concerned, agreed upon by the management of a company as a goal for performance during a specified future period.

budget, advertising

That portion of the budget of a business which concerns itself with the plans and anticipated expenditures for advertising.

budget, cash

A budget of estimated cash receipts and cash disbursements.

budget, materials

A written plan of the purchases and stores which will be needed by a business in order to meet the anticipated requirements established by the production budget.

budget, production

That portion of the budget of a business which is concerned with plans and anticipated expenditures for the production or manufacture of its products.

budget, sales

That portion of the budget of a business which is concerned with plans and anticipated expenditures for sales.

budget account

A method of credit financing in which an upper limit is placed on the amount of credit permitted. The limit is based on the size of the equal monthly payments which the customer decides he can make.

budget calendar

A calendar which provides for each step in the process of assembling estimates for the budget. For example, the preparation of sales estimates must be made in time for other departments to coordinate their plans with the sales estimates.

budget deficit

An excess of expenditures over revenues.

budget department

> The department responsible for the preparation of statements of anticipated operations in monetary terms for a business firm.

budget surplus

> An excess of revenues over expenditures.

budget variance

> The difference between budgeted costs and actual costs.

budgetary control

> The carrying out or directing of plans and expenditures as charted in the budget.

budgeting

> The written plan of anticipated incomes and expenditures of a business for a specified future period.

buffer

> Electronic memory which holds data until a certain task is finished. Limited, temporary storage.

bug

> An error in a computer program.

building codes

> State and local regulations relating to the minimum physical requirements allowed in the construction and repair of buildings.

built-in stabilizers

Also called automatic stabilizers. Characteristics of an economy that work to limit extreme economic downturns without specific government intervention. Such characteristics include unemployment and welfare benefits.

bulge

In investments this term is used to refer to a relatively sharp price advance. Such an advance would be indicated by a bulge on a chart depicting price movement.

bulk sales laws

Laws designed to prevent a debtor from fraudulantly getting a large stock of goods on credit from various manufacturers, and then selling the entire stock in bulk to a single buyer and hiding the proceeds.

bulk station operator

A wholesaler whose activities are chiefly in the petroleum field.

bull

In investment and speculation this term refers to a person who believes that the value of corporate stocks will advance.

bull market

A market in which the primary trend or direction of security or commodity prices is upward with successive highs going above previous highs and successive reactions falling short of previous lows.

bullion

> Gold or silver considered as a metal without regard to its form or to any value which may be stamped upon it. Usually, bullion is in the form of bars or ingots, but it may be in the form of old coins or foreign coins.

bureaucracy

> A form of governmental organization which is characterized by division into departments managed by officials in a prescribed, procedural manner. Often used to describe the inefficiency of an administrative function or organization.

bureaucrat

> An official who works within the prescribed regulations and procedures of a bureaucracy.

burnout

> A feeling of emotional and physical exhaustion, affecting executives and employees alike, that results in poor performance and indifference to one's job.

bus

> A term used to describe the connections between electronic components; often used specifically to describe the connections between a computer's main processor and all other circuits which can send and receive signals with it.

business

Any occupation in which people, at the risk of loss seek to make money by producing commodities for sale, or by buying and selling commodities, or by hiring the services of others for utilization at a profit. Any gainful occupation for which profit is the goal and in which there is a risk of loss.

business, service

Any business engaged in such things as maintenance, supplies, installation and repairs as contrasted with a business dealing in tangible commodities.

business administration

The managing of the affairs of a business.

business communications

The various forms of oral and written messages used by a business in the conduct of its affairs.

business conditions

Any circumstances or external factors which modify the nature, existence or occurrence of business activities. The environment in which business operated at any particular point in time.

business cycle

A recurring sequence of changes in business activity. Following a period of prosperity, business activity declines through a recession to a low point, called a depression. A period of recovery then follows when business becomes more and more active until prosperity is restored and the cycle is completed.

business law

    The same as commercial law. See definition of commercial law.

business trust

    Also known as a Massachussets trust. A system under which owners place their investments in the hands of a board of trustees who manage the investment for the benefit of the owners or for a third party.

buy in

    A stock exchange policy where the seller of securities is responsible for the additional expenses incurred by a buyer when the seller does not deliver the securities on time. Also means joining a business venture.

buy out

    To purchase all the assets of a firm or organization.

buyer

    A consumer. Also an employee whose work is to buy goods for a business firm.

buyer's market

    The condition which exists when, under competition, the schedules of supply and demand are such that market prices are at a relatively low level, giving the buyers an advantage. A time when sellers are disposed to accept a low price rather than fail to dispose of goods and services, and buyers are disposed to retain their money rather than acquire goods and services at anything other than a low price.

buying, forward

    A policy of purchasing in large amounts at infrequent intervals as distinguished from hand-to-mouth buying.

buying, reciprocal

The act of purchasing from vendors who are customers as distinguished from vendors who are not customers.

buying habits

The observable way that buyers or consumers behave when purchasing goods and services.

buying on margin

The same as marginal trading. See definition of marginal trading.

buying power

The value of a specific monetary unit in terms of the amount of commodities or services that can be bought with it. Also, the expendable income of a specific group or class of purchasers.

buzzwords

Words or terms used commonly among members of an occupational group, not necessarily understood by others.

by-laws

The framework of rules under which the board of directors of a corporation will operate. Adopting a set of by-laws is one of the first acts of a board of directors of a newly created corporation.

by-product

A product resulting as an incident of the manufacture of some other product. In the production of lignite coal, for example, some of the by-products are coal-tar, dyes, and ammonia salts.

byte

A collection of a sequence of bits (usually 8) used to represent a character in computer code.

C

CAD/CAM

    Acronym for computer assisted device/computer assisted manufacture. The use of computers for design and control of industrial processes.

C.A.F.

    Abbreviation for cost and freight. A selling price of merchandise which includes the cost of goods and the freight to the buyer's store or warehouse.

cafeteria benefits

    A program which allows employees to individualize their company benefit plan by choosing a combination of desired benefits, and eliminating less desirable ones.

call

    A demand by a corporation for stock payment when the stock is not paid in full. Also, a corporation's act of retiring a bond or preferred stock in accordance with the terms under which it was issued.

call money

    Money loaned by banks to brokers, which is subject to call or demand payment at the discretion of the lenders.

call price

> The price paid by a corporation retiring securities in whole or in part before maturity date.

call-in time

> Compensation received by an employee who is called to work on a holiday or a day off and finds less than a full day's work available.

calls and puts

> See definition of puts and calls.

canned sales talk

> A complete sales presentation which salespeople commit to memory and use verbatim before prospects.

canvassing

> The act of going through a sales territory for such purposes as finding prospects or soliciting sales, subscriptions, advertising or the like.

capital

> An aggregation of economic goods used to promote the production of other goods instead of being valuable solely for purposes of immediate enjoyment or consumption. Produced goods to be used for further production.

capital, circulating

> Current assets such as cash, accounts receivable and inventory, undergoing more or less constant turnover.

capital, fixed

> Assets such as land, buildings, machinery and equipment, not undergoing a fairly constant turnover.

capital, fluid

> The same as liquid capital. See definition of liquid capital.

capital, quick

> The same as liquid capital. See definition of liquid capital.

capital asset

> Any asset with a life of more than one year that is not bought and sold during the ordinary course of doing business.

capital budget

> A budget related to the acquisition of capital assets. A capital budget is normally prepared annually.

capital expenditure

> The spending of funds to acquire a capital asset.

capital gain

> The amount of profit realized from the sale of a capital asset such as the sale of real estate or stock.

capital gains tax

> A special income tax which allows the taxpayer who has realized a long-term capital gain a relative tax advantage. The capital gains tax is lower than the regular income tax.

capital goods

> The tools of production. Produced goods used for the further production of wealth.

capital investment

> The spending of funds to acquire a capital asset whose benefits will be realized in future periods.

capital stock

> The outstanding shares of a corporation representing ownership interest.

capital structure

> The kinds of securities which make up the capitalization of a corporation.

capitalist

> One who has capital, especially a person who has or controls a large amount of accumulated wealth used in business. A person who owns a business operating under the capitalistic system.

capitalization

> The total outstanding stocks and bonds of a corporation.

capitalize

> To discount or convert future income into present value. A method of evaluating the present worth of something by multiplying the net annual income by a figure representing future years of income. The actual number of years will depend on the age, condition and location of the property.

career counseling

>Professional guidance in training for and attaining one's occupational goals.

cargo

>Freight. The lading or freight of a transportation facility.

carrier

>In office management, a carrier is someone or something which transports messages and things. In transportation, the same definition holds. In insurance, the company assuming a risk is called a carrier.

carrier, common

>See definition of common carrier.

carrier, private

>A transportation company engaged in handling freight on a contract basis rather than for the public in general.

carrying charge

>The amount by which an installment sales price exceeds the cash price of a product.

cartel

>A combination of business firms formed for the purpose of attaining some degree of a monopoly power by regulating purchasing, production, and marketing of goods of member firms.

cash

cash

> Money, negotiable money orders, checks, and balances on deposit with banks after deducting outstanding checks.

cash, petty

> A separate fund set up by a business for the purpose of paying small bills as they arise.

cash budget

> A schedule showing the cash receipts, cash disbursements and net cash of a company over a specified period of time. An effective tool for cash management and forecasting.

cash cycle

> A measurement of the time it takes for cash to flow in and out of the company. For example, the length of time between the use of cash to purchase materials used in production and the collection of payment from the sale of the finished product to the customer.

cash disbursements

> The cash payments made by a company.

cash discount

> A discount given for prompt payment. An allowance made by the seller of goods to the buyer on condition that the bill be paid within a specified time.

cash flow

> The net income of a corporation plus bookkeeping deductions which are not paid out in actual money, such as depreciation, depletion amortization and reserves. Cash flow is a yardstick of a company's ability to pay dividends and to finance expansion from self-generated sources.

cash forecasting

> A cash flow projection that enables management to understand what is happening with cash and to plan and predict what is going to happen with respect to cash for a specified period of time in the future.

cash journal

> A separate accounting journal in which is recorded cash receipts and cash disbursements of a business.

cash receipts

> Money received by a business from a variety of sources, such as cash sales, interest, dividend earnings, collections and the like.

cash surrender value

> The amount an insurance company will pay if the insured surrenders his or her policy. A non-forfeiture privilege in life insurance policies, other than term, guaranteeing the insured receipt of a stated share of the total reserve if the policy lapses.

cash value

> The same as cash surrender value. See definition of cash surrender value.

cashier's check

A certified check drawn on a bank by itself and signed by an authorized bank official. Can be sold to customers or used to pay the bank's own obligations.

casualty

In insurance this term refers to an unfortunate accident or occurrence other than loss from fire, the transportation of goods or death. For example, automobile, accident and health, public liability, and worker's compensation are classified as casualty insurance risks.

caveat emptor

"Let the buyer beware." An expression referring to a doctrine that it is up to the buyer to protect oneself against unscrupulous sellers.

C.B.D.

Abbreviation for cash before delivery. Goods which are paid for before they are delivered to the consumer.

centralized data processing

See data processing, centralized.

CEO

See definition of chief executive officer.

certificate of convenience and necessity

A written authorization by a state, granting permission to a public utility to do business within a defined geographical area.

certificate of deposit (CD)

    A negotiable instrument issued by a bank or other financial institution which offers a special rate of interest in exchange for a deposit of a certain duration.

certificate of incorporation

    Also called articles of incorporation and corporation charter. A statement submitted to a designated state official, describing the purposes of the corporation and the names, addresses and number of shares held by each of the founders.

certified check

    A personal check that has been guaranteed by a bank as to signature and amount, and is generally regarded as being as good as cash.

certified public accountant (C.P.A.)

    A person who has met certain requirements in education and in experience in the field of accounting and who has passed a state examination in this field.

cestui que trust

    A beneficiary.

CFO

    See definition of chief financial officer.

chain, voluntary

    A network of stores in which the management is bound together by a common agreement as distinguished from a corporate chain which is defined elsewhere.

chain store

>A group of retail stores, essentially of the same type, centrally owned and with some degree of centalized control of operation. There are local, regional and national chains. The U.S. Bureau of the Census defines any group of eleven or more such stores a chain.

chaining

>This term refers to the manner of linking records to one another in a computer database.

chairman of the board

>The presiding officer of the board of directors of a corporation.

Chamber of Commerce

>An organization providing information and promotional data related to the economic progress of the community and affecting all its industries. Members consist of representatives of all or nearly all industries and businesses in the community, including the professions.

channel

>Any communications line between a computer and an external device.

channels of distribution

>The routes a product follows as it moves from producer to ultimate consumer.

Chapter 11

>A section of the Bankruptcy Reform Act of 1978 which supervises the reorganization of an insolvent corporation into a new corporation consisting of the old owners and creditors.

character reference

    A statement supplied by employers, acquaintances, schools, and other objective sources, testifying to a person's character.

charge account

    A credit arrangement whereby a customer is permitted to charge purchases and to pay for them according to some predetermined plan.

charge plan

    A credit agreement or arrangement between a buyer and seller. The method or plan adopted by a company whereby credit will be granted.

charge-offs

    The writing off of a bad debt on the records of a business because payment has not and probably will not be received.

chart

    A graphic representation using such things as lines, bars, or curves in order to show fluctuations of something variable such as prices.

charter

    The same as certificate of incorporation. See definition of certificate of incorporation.

check

    A negotiable instrument, payable on demand, which is drawn on a bank for payment of a specified sum of money to a designated person or bearer.

check, cashier's

> A check which is drawn on the bank that issues it, used by persons who are dealing with a business firm who may be unwilling to accept a personal check.

check, certified

> A check drawn by a depositor and guaranteed for payment by a duly authorized officer of the drawee bank.

check, post-dated

> A check dated later than the date on which the check was written. The check cannot be cashed until the date on it.

check, stop-payment

> A check which cannot be cashed due to an order written by the payee notifying the bank not to honor the payment.

check, traveler's

> A special type of check sold through banks by such companies such as the American Express Company, used by persons who do not wish to carry large sums of money with them when away from their own banking facilities.

check register

> Also called the cash disbursements journal. An accounting record of vouchers payable, cash and discounts on purchases.

chief executive officer (CEO)

> The top-level officer in a corporation, usually the president or chairperson of the board of directors.

chief financial officer (CFO)

>The top-level financial officer in a corporation.

chip

>Sometimes used as a synonym for integrated circuit or semi-conductor. A tiny memory device made of a material called silicon. See also circuit, integrated circuit and semiconductor.

C.I.F.

>Abbreviation for costs, insurance, freight. A selling price which includes the cost of goods, the cost of insuring the shipment, and the cost of freight to the buyer's place of business.

circuit

>One single cell or electronic switch on a chip. A large chip contains more than 60,000 separate circuits on an area smaller than a child's fingernail. Also used to refer to circuit board.

circuit board

>A collection of chips on a single assembly, usually designed to perform a specific function.

circular industry

>A combining of enterprises which tends to unite industries which manufacture products alike, complementary in nature, or which can readily be sold in the same market.

civil law

>The system of law which is based on codes. The codes are compilations of laws, rules and regulations.

Civil Rights Act

A U.S. law prohibiting discrimination in employment on the basis of race, color, religion or national origin.

claim

A demand for payment or adjustment for injury, damage, misrepresentation, or defective goods and services.

claim letter

A letter requesting some kind of refund or adjustment for errors that occurred in a business transaction because of misunderstanding, misrepresentation, damaged or otherwise unsatisfactory goods or services.

classified advertising

A type of advertising which appears in columns of a publication under fixed headings, usually in alphabetical order.

class rate

A charge in transportation assigned a class or a group of analogous articles.

clearing house

A voluntary association of banks created to facilitate the clearing of checks, drafts, notes and other items among members.

clerical work

Routine business work performed by clerks, such as handling mail, keeping simple records, operating simple office machines and filing.

clincher

> Any special inducement used in the last stages of trying to motivate people to buy or take some desired action.

clip-sheet

> A series of features and background material sent daily by a news or picture syndicate to its newspaper clients for use as the newspaper sees fit.

clock rate

> The speed at which a computer's central processor can send out individual electronic signals. Most microcomputers have clock rates around 4MHz, four million cycles per second. See also bandwidth.

close, the

> The final steps taken by a salesperson making a presentation of a product in which the salesperson tries to get the prospect to commit himself to buy. Also, in investments this expression refers to the end of a trading session when all trades are officially declared as having been executed "at or on the close."

closed-end investment trust

> See definition of investment trust.

closed-end question

> In marketing, a survey question which requires the respondent to choose an answer from a given selection of responses, as distinguished from an open-end question which is defined elsewhere.

closed shop

> A business which employs only union members in good standing.

closing

> In accounting, this term refers to the act of summarizing the books at the end of a period as a step toward preparing the financial statement.

COBOL

> Acronym for common business oriented language. The most popular language for large computers running financial applications for business.

C.O.D.

> Abbreviation for cash on delivery. Goods which are paid for at the time they are delivered to the consumer.

code

> Any instruction written for a computer in any language. All forms of programming are known as code.

coding

> The act of preparing a list of successive operations in order for a computer to solve a problem.

coinage

> The government process of stamping a piece of metal, certifying its weight and fineness.

coinage, free

> The condition existing when the owner of bullion is at liberty to have it coined on the same terms as the government.

coinsurance clause

An insurance clause establishing that the carrier will pay a loss in the proportion that the insurance carrier bears to the value of the property.

cold call

In sales, contacting a prospective customer for a sale or appointment without giving advance notice.

collateral

Something of value which is used as a pledge to secure the repayment of a loan.

collection

The securing of payments from customers who did not pay cash at the time of purchase.

collection letter

A business letter or series of letters designed to help in the task of collecting overdue credit accounts.

collection procedure

The method established for securing payments of amounts due from credit customers.

collective bargaining

The process by which the representatives of labor bargain with representatives of management over the terms of labor contracts or agreements.

collusive bidding

> The act by which two or more companies submit bids for a job according to prior agreement.

co-maker

> A person who signs a note in addition to the borrower to give extra security to the loan. The co-maker is jointly and severally liable with the borrower for repayment.

combination, conglomerate

> The linking or joining together of corporations from different industries.

combination, corporate

> The linking or joining together of corporations either formally or informally.

combination, horizontal

> The joining together or linking of business enterprises which market the same kind of products or close substitutes.

combination, vertical

> The joining together or linking of two or more companies engaged in different but related levels of production or distribution of a product such as a combination of a raw material producer with a processor.

combination sale

> The sale of a second item or items in conjunction with an established product at an attractive combination price. Usually the second product is a new one which is sold in combination with a well-known product.

combined statement

>An integrated income statement or integrated balance sheet of a parent company with its subsidiaries.

commerce

>The interchange of goods between traders.

commercial

>That which has to do with the interchange of commodities. Having to do with business intercourse. Also, an advertising message presented over radio or television.

commercial art

>The kind of artwork used in advertising, the purpose of which is to increase demand for products and services through pictorial representations.

commercial law

>The legal rules which relate to mercantile transactions. The body of legal rules governing business intercourse.

commercial paper

>Unsecured, short-term promissory notes that are sold by businesses to commercial paper houses who, in turn, sell them to other financial institutions and corporations.

commercial paper house

>An organization which specializes in retailing short-term promissory notes of businesses to banks, investors and other purchasers interested in this type of investment.

commission

A compensation plan by which a salesman receives a percentage of his sales revenue as all or part of his income. The amount charged by a securities broker for buying or selling securities for a client.

commission house

The same as selling agent. See definition of selling agent.

commission merchant

An agent who transacts business in his own name, usually exercising physical control over the goods consigned but not sold to him, and who negotiates the sale of such goods under instructions issued by his principal.

committee

A group of persons appointed to take action on some particular business matter for an organization.

committee organization

A type of business organization in which a group of executives acting jointly perform the various management functions.

commitment fee

A lending fee charged by financial institutions for a line of credit.

commodity

Anything which has value and is therefore salable. Everything which is movable that is bought and sold, such as wares, merchandise and produce.

commodity approach

> An approach to marketing which analyzes the subject by the commodities or goods involved: capital goods, industrial goods, and consumer goods. Other approaches are the institutional approach and the functional approach which are defined elsewhere.

commodity exchange

> A place where buyers and sellers of staple commodities such as wheat, corn, cotton, sugar and coffee are brought together.

commodity rate

> A charge assigned for shipping specified commodities from and to stations of origin and destination.

common carrier

> A company which offers transportation services, including storage, communication, and other supplementary services to the general public.

common law

> The system of law which is based on precedents established by decisions in past cases of a similar nature.

common stock

> Ownership stock. A type of stock sold by a corporation to raise long-term capital, giving stockholders a share of ownership (and usually a voice) in the financial destiny of the company.

communications

> The exchange of ideas by means of speech, writing or signal.

community of interests

> A situation where two or more corporations are controlled by the same stockholders. In the past this has sometimes been a form of combination which operated in restraint of trade.

company

> A business organization of persons who, at the risk of loss, seek to make money in a commercial venture.

company man

> A slang term for an employee with great loyalty to the company.

company store

> A store owned and operated by a business for the convenience of its employees.

comparable worth

> Providing equal compensation for different jobs that are considered as having the same value or worth to an employer.

comparative advantage

> A situation in which a person, business, or nation has relative advantage over parties with whom it trades in producing a given product or performing an economic activity. Such an advantage should economically be exploited in order to receive the most return for effort.

compatible

> A similarity between computers such that equipment and programs for one can be used with the other.

compensating balance

> A bank account whose earnings based on average daily balances offsets any bank fees charged for the maintenance of the account.

compensation

> The income received as pay for services rendered. The sum of wages, salaries, and supplements to wages and salaries which represent, from the employer's viewpoint, the direct cost of labor.

compensation, monetary

> Payment in money to a person for some act or service rendered.

compensation, unemployment

> An income, usually paid weekly, to workers who are both willing and able to work but who are unable to get a job. A program sponsored by the U.S. government under the Federal Social Security Act of 1935 which assists the states in providing compensation for the unemployed.

compensatory damage

> An amount given or awarded to an injured party for injury or damage sustained.

competition

> The act of striving for something that is sought by others at the same time. A market situation in which there are many informed and independent buyers and suppliers of the same economic good or service and in which the price is free from government interference.

competition, imperfect

> A situation in an economy involving a departure from perfect competition due to inadequacy of market information, restraint on freedom of action of buyers and sellers, legal restrictions on entry into the field, product differentiation, or the like.

competition, perfect

> An idealized condition or model world of competition in which sellers and buyers are so numerous and small that none controls enough supply or demand to affect price.

competition, pure

> The same as perfect competition. See definition of competition, perfect.

competition, unfair

> A term applied generally to a situation in which dishonest or fraudulent rivalry exists in a trade or industry.

competitor

> A person or business attempting to offer a better or cheaper commodity or service. A rival for a common business market.

compiler

> A program which converts another program in a high-level language such as BASIC, to assembly language for a computer's microprocessor, line by line as the program is run.

complimentary close

> The closing of a business letter after the final paragraph and before the signature of the writer. Such expressions as "Yours truly," and "Sincerely yours," are complimentary closes.

composition

> In commercial law this refers to an agreement by creditors to accept a stated percentage of their claims as a complete discharge in order to avoid long, costly proceedings in bankruptcy.

comprehensive coverage

> A blanket protection under an insurance contract for practically all risks involving property, such as combined protection for losses due to fire, theft, and casualty.

comptroller, controller

> A person responsible for budgeting, accounting, statistical reporting and internal auditing. The first spelling usually used in government; the second in industry.

computer

> Any machine or device which can perform mathematical calculations.

computing

> The act of determining information through calculations.

concealment

> The witholding of material facts from an insurer in the negotiation of an insurance contract or in the making of a claim.

concern

An organization or establishment engaged in some form of business.

conditional sale

A sale in which the buyer is given possession of the goods, but title is reserved expressly in the seller as security for the buyer's payment.

conference

A consultation, discussion or exchange of views.

conflict of interest

A situation that arises when personal influences enter into one's ability to be impartial or act in the best interests of one's job.

conflict resolution

A management strategy that aims to resolve disagreements in a constructive manner rather than a destructive one, based on the belief that conflict can be beneficial to an organization if handled in the proper way.

consideration

Anything of value requested by the promisor as an acceptable exchange for his or her promise. One of the basic elements of a valid contract.

consignee

The recipient of merchandise which has been shipped on consignment.

consignment

> The transfer of goods, without transfer of title, from a seller or vendor to a consignee who usually sells the goods for a commission and remits the net proceeds to the consignor.

consignor

> The owner who ships merchandise to a party on consignment.

consolidation

> The same as amalgamation. See definition of amalgamation.

conspiracy to restrain trade

> An act by which two or more persons or businesses seek, usually through unlawful means, to create a monopoly, to control prices or to suppress competition.

constant

> A mathematical figure or magnitude which does not change its value in a given situation.

consumer

> A buyer of goods.

consumer, ultimate

> One who buys goods and services for one's own personal or household wants. One who uses the goods one buys for one's own satisfaction rather than for profit or investment.

consumer finance

> The granting of credit to ultimate consumers by retailers, banks, and other lending agencies.

consumer goods

> Materials destined for use by the ultimate household consumer without further commercial processing. Consumer goods are divided into three categories: Convenience goods, shopping goods and specialty goods. These are defined elsewhere.

consumer motivation

> The field of study which explains why consumers act the way they do in buying goods and in patronizing certain businesses.

consumer price index (CPI)

> An economic indicator published monthly by the Bureau of Labor Statistics which measures changes in the average cost of goods and services purchased by consumers. The CPI is used most often as a measure of inflation.

consumer survey

> A form of market research to establish who uses a product, what influences the purchase of specific products, how products are used, and how they are purchased.

consumption

> The use of goods and services for the satisfaction of human desires. Also the use of goods and services for productive purposes, as when raw materials are consumed in the production of the finished product.

contingent liability

>A loss that is likely to occur but which has not yet occurred as of the end of the accounting period. Such losses should be disclosed in the body of the financial statements if estimable, or in the notes to the financial statements.

continuous form

>This refers to output from a computer's printer. Paper is fed into the computer in one continuous sheet to increase speed of the output.

contract

>A legally binding agreement between two or more parties in which, for a consideration, one or more of the parties agree to do something.

contract, conditional sales

>An installment sales agreement which provides that title remains with the seller until full payment is made. If installments are not paid when due, the holder of the contract may repossess the goods.

contract, illegal

>An agreement which is either against the best interests of society or is declared illegal by statute.

contract carrier

>The same as private carrier. See definition of carrier, private.

contracts, tying

>Sales agreements which force a buyer to take certain undesirable merchandise in order to secure the particular merchandise he or she wants.

contribution margin

> The difference between a company's net sales and its variable costs per unit.

control

> The regulation of some phase of business or economic life.

control, flow

> The coordination of men, machines, tools and materials in a production process, especially when a company manufactures for stock as distinguished from manufacturing only after customers' orders have been received.

control, inventory

> The procedures which are established by a firm to regulate the proper and expeditious handling of inventory.

control, materials

> The securing and providing of needed materials, parts, and supplies of the right kind, quality and amount at the right place and time.

control, order

> The coordination of men, machines, tools and materials in production when a company manufactures orders as they are received from customers.

control, quantity

> A system of supervision used by a business to limit the amount of goods-in-process to the amount needed at any given time.

control, sales

A system of supervision involving the use of records, statistics and personal contact for the purpose of exercising control over marketing policies and plans.

control unit

The part of the CPU that monitors the operations of the computer.

convenience goods

Those things which a customer purchases frequently, finds almost anywhere, and acquires with a minimum of effort.

conversion parity

Value of a bond based on converting it into a stock rather than holding it as a bond. Parity is obtained by dividing the conversion price of stock into the conversion price of the bond and multiplying the quotient by the market price of the stock.

conversion privilege

The right of a policy holder under stipulated conditions to change from one type of insurance policy to another.

conveyance

In commercial law this refers to the transfer of property from one party to another.

cooling-off period

A period of time agreed on in a labor contract during which no overt action will be taken by either party in a labor dispute.

cooperative (co-op)

A voluntary business enterprise organized by a group of people in order to serve their own needs. Each member has an equal amount of control, and profit is distributed to members in proportion to their patronage. See also advertising, cooperative.

cooperative, farmer's

A cooperative formed by farmers usually in the marketing of agricultural products where it is possible through the joint venture to control the supply of products and also to realize some of the income which otherwise would go to middlemen.

co-owner

One of two or more persons who owns something jointly or equally, such as a partner in a business firm.

copy

The text of an advertisement. The main body of writing in an advertisement which is intended to create attention, invite interest, give information and promote action. Any written material prepared for a printer.

copyright

An exclusive right to control the publishing and distributing of a particular work, such as a book, a movie, a piece of music, or a work of art.

corner the market

An expression in investments which refers to the gaining of control over the price of a stock or commodity by acquiring a large enough block of it. A corner exists when so little stock is available that those who sold short are forced to buy at a price set arbitrarily high.

corporate chain

A network of stores which is owned by a single corporation.

corporate personality

The image of a corporation to employees, stockholders, customers and others interested in it or of interest to it.

corporate seal

The official stamp of a corporation.

corporation

A type of business organization. An artificial being possessing properties granted it by legal charter, distinct from those who compose it.

corporation, alien

A legal entity operating in a country but chartered by a foreign government.

corporation, closed

A legal entity whose stock is not offered for sale to the general public. A corporation owned and controlled by a relatively small number of stockholders, the stock of which is not available to the general public.

corporation, domestic

A legal entity that operates in the state which granted its charter.

corporation, foreign

    A legal entity doing business in any state other than the state which granted its charter.

corporation, nonstock

    A legal entity which does not issue stock because it is a not-for-profit company organized by a charitable, educational, governmental, or religious group.

corporation, not-for-profit

    A legal entity which does not distribute profit to its owners or founders. A social, charitable, religious, educational or public corporation formed for motives other than profit.

corporation, open

    A legal entity whose stock is sold to the general public and which makes public its complete financial report at least once a year.

corporation, private

    A legal entity which is owned and operated by private individuals as distinguished from a public corporation.

corporation, public

    A legal entity which is established and operated for governmental purposes or for the administration of public affairs by a city, state or federal government.

corporation charter

>The same as certificate of incorportion. See definition of certificate of incorporation.

corporation income tax

>A levy by a federal or state government on the profits of a corporation.

correlation

>In statistics this refers to a close relationship between two groups of data. The closer the relationship, either positive or negative, the higher the degree of correlation.

correspondent bank

>A bank which acts as an agent for other banks by providing various banking services.

cost

>The money-outlay required to get a commodity or service. The money-outlay to get a valuable income.

cost, distribution

>The cost or expense which occurs in the marketing of a product.

cost, fixed

>A cost such as rental of a building which does not fluctuate in proportion to the level of production or of operation.

cost, marginal

> The increase in the total cost of production resulting from the addition of one unit of output.

cost, unit

> The cost of a single product or service including variable cost and the amount of fixed cost allocated to the product or service.

cost, variable

> The portion of a unit cost which changes, increases, or decreases as the output changes, increases, or decreases.

cost control, accounting

> The supervision and regulation of costs through a system of records which will establish accountability for them. Employment of current, pertinent, and concise accounting and statistical reports to reveal how people are discharging their responsibilities.

cost control, operational

> The supervision and regulation of costs in an enterprise through personal observation and supervision of operations as distinguished from accounting cost control.

cost of capital

> The cost of the long-term debt and equity capital to the company. It is expressed as a percent, and used to determine acceptable rates of return on capital projects.

cost of goods sold

> The accounting estimate of the purchase price of goods sold by a firm during a particular period. In order to arrive at this figure, the company must first determine the inventory on hand at the beginning of the period. To this is added the cost of freight and net purchases. The sum of these three represents the cost of merchandise available for sale. From this is subtracted the inventory on hand at the end of the period. The remainder is cost of goods sold.

cost of living

> A term used to refer to the cost of purchasing goods and services by consumers intent upon maintaining a certain standard of existence. It is usually used in comparative instances, such as a rise or fall in the cost of living this year as compared to last year.

cost-benefit analysis

> The process of determining which of several alternatives is best for achieving a particular objective. It consists of comparing the alternatives' expected costs and benefits and choosing that alternative with the smallest cost-benefit ratio.

cost-of-living increase

> Also, cost-of-living raise. A salary increase based on a cost-of-living index (commonly, the Consumer Price Index) as distinguished from a merit increase which is defined elsewhere.

cost-plus contract

> A contract that calls for payment computed by taking the total cost of producing or supplying the item and adding to it a percentage of the total production cost.

cost-plus pricing

A method of determining sales price by adding a percentage of the total cost of goods to the cost. The percentage is expected to cover additional expenses to the company and profits.

cost-push inflation

A situation where increasing labor costs causes firms to increase prices charged to consumers.

costs, direct

Costs which can be traced and allocated to a specific product or lot of production, used in cost accounting. For example, the wage of a machine operator who works on a specific product is a direct cost of that product.

costs, historical

Costs which are accumulated from past records.

costs, indirect

Costs which cannot be directly traced or allocated to a specific product or lot of production such as the rent of a factory in which multiple products are produced.

costs, standard

Predetermined or precomputed costs which serve as the basis of cost control and as a measure of efficiency when compared with actual costs.

counterfeit money

> Money made to resemble real money and used with intent to defraud.

counter-offer

> A reply which does not conform to the exact terms of an original offer and, therefore, does not constitute an acceptance which binds a contract.

coupon

> A certificate entitling its bearer to something of value, such as a certificate attached to a bond entitling its bearer to interest or a certificate obtained from an advertisement entitling its bearer to a premium.

C.P.A.

> Abbreviation for certified public accountant. See definition of certified public accountant.

CP/M

> Control program for microprocessors. An operating system popular with microcomputers. See also operating system.

CPM

> Abbreviation for critical path method. A network diagramming technique that places emphasis on time, cost, and the completion of events.

CPU

>Abbreviation for central processing unit. Controls the operations of the computer system and consists of primary storage, an ALU, and a control unit.

creative financing

>An alternative method of financing a real estate purchase without using a conventional fixed-rate mortgage.

credit

>The amount of indebtedness one may incur for goods and services. In accounting, a credit is an entry posted to the right side of a ledger.

credit, documentary

>An account payable in which the credit sale is based on the promise of the buyer as expressed through the medium of a written instrument.

credit, intermediate

>Credit which is established for a period longer than short-term credit (one year or less) and shorter than long-term credit (ten years or more).

credit card

>A card which gives its holder the right to purchase goods and services on account.

credit letter

>A written communication usually emanating from the credit and collection department of a company, dealing with some aspect of the

recipient's credit such as an acknowledgement of a request for credit, refusal of credit, or the like.

credit line

An amount of credit a lender makes available for borrowing.

credit rating

An appraisal or classification of an individual's or firm's ability to meet financial obligations.

credit report

A report available from credit agencies that includes information on customers such as credit accounts maintained, payment history, outstanding debts, etc.

credit transaction

A business transaction in which goods, services, or other values are exchanged for the promise to pay for them in the future.

credit union

A cooperative employee savings and loan association which promotes thrift and makes loans to its members.

creditor

A person to whom a debt is owed by another person or corporation who is known as the debtor.

creditor, general

A person to whom a debt is owed who has no claim to preferential treatment in the settlement of a bankruptcy proceedings as distinguished from a preferential creditor.

creditor, preferred

A person to whom a debt is owed who has a claim to payment prior to the general run of creditors. For example, an employee with wages due has a prior claim over a general creditor.

creditor beneficiary

A third party to whom a promisee owes a debt. If the promisee contracts with another to pay the debt, the creditor beneficiary can enforce the promise.

creeping inflation

The slow and steady rise in the general price level, about 2.5 percent a year.

CRT

Abbreviation for cathode ray tube. A term for the most common type of video display, similar to that of a television tube.

cum pf

Abbreviation for cumulative preferred stock. See definition of stock, cumulative.

currency

Money circulated as a medium of exchange, issued and authorized by a government through law.

cursor

> The small blinking light, underline, or other visual marker on a video display which shows where the program is focused at any point in time.

curve

> A line connecting specific points on a chart, representing a trend or average.

curve, deviation

> A line on a chart which shows the variation from the central tendency or standard.

custom manufacture

> The production of goods to customer specifications as distinguished from standard manufacture which is defined elsewhere.

customer

> A buyer of goods or services, usually on a regular basis.

customs duty

> A tax levied on imported goods.

cycles

> As related to business, a cycle is a round or series of economic events that reappear at periodic intervals. The four phases of the business cycle are: prosperity, decline, depression and recovery.

cyclical variation

> A change or deviation from the normal or expected business cycle.

D

daisywheel

    A small print wheel containing letters and numerals which is attached to a computer printer or electronic typewriter.

data

    Facts about the real world. Raw data must be converted into machine-readable data before it can be entered into a computer system as input. See also information. Also, a group of collected facts from which information can be garnered or conclusions drawn about a particular subject.

data flow diagram

    A graphic representation of the movement of data through a system. See also flowchart.

data processing

    The storage, manipulation and retrieval of data by computers.

data processing, centralized

> Data processing performed by a single computer (usually a mainframe) within a company, as distinguished from decentralized or distributed data processing which are defined elsewhere.

data processing, decentralized

> Data processing performed by individual departments within a company by the use of several independent computer facilities. This is distinguished from centralized or distributed data processing which are defined elsewhere.

data processing, distributed

> A data processing system that incorporates both centralized and decentralized data processing by using a central data base with numerous departmental and/or individual terminals having access to the central facility. See also data processing, centralized and data processing, decentralized.

database management system

> A software package that allows users full usage of a database system, including provisions for creating files, updating files, querying the database and printing management reports.

date of record

> A date on or before which the stock owner must be shown on company books to receive a declared dividend.

dating

> A modification of the usual terms of sales, whereby the time of payment is extended to give preferential terms.

dating codes

    A method of marking price tags with numbers or letter or both in order to keep a record of the age of goods.

day care

    Providing for the care of pre-school children in a center specifically organized for that purpose, while both parents work. Some employers offer day care benefits to reduce the financial burden of their employees with small children.

dead-end position

    Also, dead-end job. A job that is perceived as presenting no opportunity for advancement.

deadheading

    Passing over an employee with seniority in order to promote a lower level employee with greater qualifications.

deadwood

    A slang reference to those individuals of a company who, for one reason or another, have lost their motivation and are no longer productive members of the firm. Many times, in a move to cut back on the payroll, a company will look to prune away any "deadwood" employees in the organization.

dealer

    A person who is engaged in buying, selling or trading.

death benefits

>The proceeds received by a beneficiary from an insurance policy upon the death of the insured.

debasement

>A cheapening of the value of coin by reducing the amount of precious metal contained in it.

debenture

>See definition of bond, debenture.

debit

>In accounting, a debit is an entry posted on the left side of a ledger.

debt

>An obligation of one person to pay money, goods or service to another person as a result of a previous agreement.

debtor

>A person who owes another person payment for goods or services or for money loaned.

debug

>To eliminate flaws from a computer or computer program.

decentralizing

> The spreading of authority and of responsibilities from a central office to branches. The delegating of authority from a centralized point to a number of areas or localities.

decile

> See definition of quartile.

decision tree

> A graphic representation of various possible alternatives, and results that follow from a sequence of possible choices.

decline

> A stage of the business cycle often called recession, characterized by business apprehension. Production slows down, investors grow wary, industry becomes reluctant to borrow, banks tighten credit, unemployment sets in, and wages go down.

decruitment

> A management strategy of moving older upper level managers into lower level and lower paying positions.

dedicated line

> A communications link, such as a telephone line, that is used for a single, specific connection, as distinguished from a line which is shared.

dedicated system

> A computer system that is used for a specific application.

deductible

> An amount which can be subtracted or taken away from a principal sum or amount.

deed

> A written document used to convey or transfer real estate from one owner to another.

deed, quitclaim

> A form of deed which transfers the interest of the grantor in real estate but does not guarantee that the grantor conveys clear title.

deed, warranty

> A form of deed which guarantees that the seller has the right to convey clear title to real estate and that the property is free from debts not specifically stated.

defalcation

> The misappropriation of money or property by a person entrusted with it.

default

> Any debt obligation which has not been honored according to its terms. Also, the value in a computer program which is in effect unless the user changes it.

defendant

> The person sued by the plaintiff.

deferred

> Anything which is postponed until a later date.

deferred asset

> The same as deferred charge. See definition of deferred charge.

deferred charge

> Also called deferred asset. In accounting, this term refers to an asset which arises through an adjustment of an expense account, the effect of which is to carry part of the expense forward into the next accounting period.

deferred compensation

> Postponement of earnings, usually until retirement, for income tax purposes. Sometimes done as part of a pension plan, the compensation received by an employee after retirement is usually taxed at a much lower rate.

deferred credit

> The same as deferred liability. See definition of deferred liability.

deferred income

> In accounting this refers to money received but not yet earned. This remains a liability until it can be claimed as income.

deferred liability

> Also called deferred credit. In accounting, this term refers to credit which arises through an adjustment of an income account, the effect of which is to carry part of the income into the next accounting period because it has not yet been earned.

deferred wage increase

A pay increase planned for a future specific date, usually negotiated in a union contract.

deficit

The net loss of a corporation because expenditures exceeded income. Also, the excess of liabilities over assets, resulting in a negative earned surplus. In budgetary control the term is used to signify a condition where obligations and expenditures exceed the standards established for control purposes.

deficit financing

When a governmental body takes in less money than it spends, making up the difference by borrowing (issuing bonds) as opposed to increasing taxes. Also called deficit spending.

deflation

The act of taking money out of circulation, resulting is a fall in prices and a rise in the purchasing power of money.

delivery, conditional

Terms or conditions accompanying the delivery of goods, which must be met or accepted before goods will be delivered.

delivery, unconditional

A delivery of goods with no terms or conditions imposed on the receiver.

demand

The entire schedule of amounts of any product which buyers will purchase at different prices during a given period of time.

demand, consumer

> The desire by an ultimate consumer, possessing the ability and willingness to pay, for a product or service offered at any specific price.

demand, elastic

> A situation which exists when a certain percent change in the price of a product results in a greater percent change in demand.

demand, inelastic

> A situation which exists when a certain percent change in the price of a product results in a lesser percent change in demand.

demand curve

> Also called demand schedule. A geometric graphic representation showing the inverse relationship between price and quantity, the fundamental law of demand. The curve shows that the higher the price rises the less will be the demand.

demand deposit

> A checking account in a bank.

demand schedule

> The same as demand curve. See definition of demand curve.

demand-pull inflation

> A situation in which a high demand for loans triggers a rise in consumer and industrial prices. This expands the money supply which in

turn creates more demand and rising prices. See also cost-push inflation.

demodulation

Converting an analog signal, such as a telephone voice or video, to a computer's digital format.

demographic characteristics

In marketing, the general traits that typify a market segment, such as age, gender, family size, education, race, religion, social class, and the like.

demonstration

A public showing of goods in order to introduce a new product, to show an application of a product not readily apparent, or to stimulate the consumer to buy.

demotion

A reduction in the grade or rank of a person employed by a business.

department

A distinct part, division, or subdivision of an organization or business.

department head

A person in charge of the business operation of a department.

departmental operation

The method of business operation carried out by a firm which is organized into a department system.

departmentalization

> The grouping together of common or homogeneous activities to form an organizational unit.

depletion

> The exhaustion of resources of any kind by the act of using them up.

deposit

> Money put in a bank, establishing a debtor-creditor relationship. A partial payment on merchandise.

deposit currency

> Checks and other credit instruments deposited with a bank as the equivalent of cash and made payable on demand. The major part of a bank's currency deposits consists of checks, money orders, and drafts rather than actual money.

depositor

> A person, proprietorship, corporations, orgnization, or association which deposits money in a bank.

depository bank

> A local bank used as a temporary place of deposit for cash receipts that will soon be transferred to another branch or bank.

depreciation

> The loss of value sustained by tangible fixed assets as a result of wear and tear, the passage of time, and the action of the elements. The

stated loss of value of a fixed asset in an accounting statement in order to adjust its value as it gradually wears out.

depreciation, double declining balance

A method of depreciation under which double the straight line rate is applied each year to the remaining unrecovered cost of the asset.

depreciation, straight-line

A method of depreciation under which the cost of the asset, less the estimated salvage value, is written off in equal annual amounts over its life.

depreciation, sum-of-the-digits

A method of depreciation under which the annual depreciation allowance is determined by the use of a fraction, the numerator being the remaining years of life of the asset at the beginning of the year and the denominator being the sum of the digits of the years of useful life at acquisition.

depreciation, unit production

A method of depreciation in which the asset is gradually reduced in terms of total units of product which will be processed by it.

depreciation, working-hours

A method of depreciation in which machine hours are substituted for years in the estimate of useful life.

depression

A stage of the business cycle during which business is at a low level of activiy, unemployment is high, wages are down, sales are slow, and production is curtailed.

deregulation

A reduction in the legislation governing a particular industry, in the interest of increasing competition in that industry.

design

The intended arrangement of materials to produce a certain result or effect. Industrial design, called structural design, refers to the design of useful products to be mass produced by machine.

design, package

The design of wrappings, cushioning material, containers, and markings to protect items from deterioration, to prevent loss and damage, to facilitate handling, to identify and to promote sales.

deskilled

A term referring to a job or jobs which have been simplified as the result of the growth of specialization. Simple tasks or jobs requiring no skill to perform.

desk-jobber

The same as drop-shipper. See definition of drop-shipper.

desterilization of reserves

Any method of increasing bank reserves, thus permitting the bank to expand loans and investments.

devaluation

To fix the value of a currency at a lower level. Also, to assess downward the value of land, machinery, or other assets.

development credit corporation

>A credit company set up by a state or community for the purpose of financing new industries.

deviation, average

>A means of measuring the spread of data above and below a central tendency. In statistics, average deviation is determined by dividing the number of cases into the sum of deviations from the average. It is not quite as accurate a measurement as standard deviation.

deviation, standard

>A means of measuring the spread of data above and below a central tendency. In statistics, standard deviation is determined by squaring the sum of deviations from the average, dividing this figure by the number of cases and taking the square root of this quotient. It is a more accurate measurement than average deviation.

differentials (shift, skill, wage)

>The increased pay rates accorded to workers who perform certain unusual or undesirable tasks.

digital

>A number system using only discrete numbers, such as 0 and 1, or 1, 2, 3, etc., without any of the possible numbers between them. Digital does not mean binary, though almost every modern digital computer does use the binary system.

diminishing returns, law of

>A principle which states that extra additions to output eventually start to become less economical if one of the factors of production remains constant. For example, if more fertilizer, labor and machinery continue

to be crowded into one acre of land (a fixed factor), the costs for additional output will gradually increase faster than the revenue.

direct access

The ability to access data regardless of its location on the disk as distinguished from sequential access. See also random access.

directive

A communication which directs a recipient to act in a certain way, used for important memoranda such as policy statements.

directors

The same as board of directors. See definition of board of directors.

disaffirmance

In law, this refers to the right of a minor to disavow a contract and to recover the money or property he or she has paid under it.

discharge

A permanent release or dismissal of a worker from employment.

disclaimer clause

A clause in a contract declaring that the seller excludes any and all warranties in connection with the transaction.

discount

A deduction from an original price which is allowed for paying promptly or in cash.

discount, bank

    A charge for a loan made by a bank and subtracted in advance.

discount, earned

    A deduction from the full price which is realized by paying cash for the goods or service within a stated period.

discount, quantity

    A deduction in price given as inducement to buyers to purchase in larger amounts.

discount, time

    The same as a cash discount. See definition of cash discount.

discount, trade

    A price reduction which is based on the kind of commercial buyer.

discount, unearned

    A deduction in price taken after the expiration of a stated discount period, and therefore one which is not due.

discount house

    An establishment which offers discounts on branded merchandise because it takes advantage of low overhead, low operating costs, high volume turnover, and little or no service.

discounted cash flow methods (DCF)

Capital budgeting technique of ranking investment projects such as the internal rate of return and net present value methods. Both take into consideration the time value of money and discount cash flows in order to compare investment projects.

discounts, chain

A series of discounts from list price. Chain discounts are generally used by a business firm as a way of announcing price changes without reprinting price lists.

discrimination

In employment, this refers to the unfair treatment of a person resulting in limited employment or advancement opportunities, on the basis of that person's sex, race, color, age, national origin, religion or physical handicap. See also reverse discrimination.

dishonor

The act of refusing to pay a promissory instrument when due or when presented for payment.

disk

A storage medium for computer files. See floppy disk, hard disk, or magnetic disk.

disk drive

A direct access device for disks. Allows user to read from and/or write on a disk which is inserted into the drive.

dispatching

>The authorizing of the manufacture of parts and quantities scheduled. Putting production work orders in to effect and transmit routing papers to the shop.

display

>Any sign or exhibit, the primary purpose of which is to remind people of the availability of a product or service.

display, point of sale

>A display which is located in a retail outlet at or near the place where the merchandise is sold.

display, window

>A display of merchandise in the show-window of a business.

disposable income

>Also, disposable personal income. The amount of money available for spending after taxes and other government payments have been deducted.

distribution

>In marketing, this term refers to moving products from producer to consumer. In statistics, the term refers to the manner in which things being measured are spread between the highest and lowest points on a scale.

distribution costs

Any expense attributed to the selling and distribution of a product, including advertising, storage, and delivery costs.

distributor

A district wholesaler representing one or more manufacturers and having rights to the distribution of specified products in his territory.

diversification

The spreading of investment risk by dividing funds among stocks and bonds of different types, in different localities, and in different industries. Also, the act of taking on new products by a business firm, especially products which will open new types of markets or will stabilize the level of production.

dividend

The distribution by a corporation of a portion of earnings or of assets to stockholders.

dividend, cumulative

A dividend which has not been paid by a corporation and which accumulates as an obligation against earnings until paid.

dividend, patronage

A dividend which is paid by a cooperative to a member on the basis of the amount the member has bought or sold through the cooperative.

dividend, stock

A dividend paid by a corporation in the form of additional shares of stock instead of cash.

documentation

> The written information that accompanies an application program or system and describes its design and how to use it.

dollar cost averaging

> A method of buying securities with fixed amounts of money at regular intervals, regardless of the current price of the securities.

donee beneficiary

> A person to whom a promisee intending to make a gift does so by buying a promise. The promisor is to render a performance directly to the donee beneficiary.

donor

> A person who gives a gift or creates a voluntary trust.

dot-matrix printer

> A common type of impact printer which forms characters using a series of dots placed in a grid format. Can provide near letter quality output.

double indemnity

> The provision in some life insurance policies that doubles the amount the insurance policy will be paid if death results from an accident.

double taxation

> Legally, the taxation of the same income as first, corporate income and second, as personal income derived from stockholders' dividends. Illegally, double taxation is the levying of taxes against the same income and for the same purpose more than once.

double time

>The payment of twice an employee's wages for hours worked overtime, Sundays, or on legal holidays.

double-name paper

>A promissory note which a holder discounts at a bank by endorsing it. Thus, the bank has two sources of repayment: the maker and the original lender who has endorsed it.

Dow Jones Averages

>The Dow Jones Averages consist of four different averages of stock prices that serve as a measure of the stock market as a whole. They include 30 industrial stocks (the Industrial Average), 20 transportation stocks, 15 utility stocks, and a composite average of the three.

download

>Same as dump. See definition for dump.

downtime

>A unit of time when a computer or peripheral is not functioning.

draft

>The same as a commercial draft. See definition of draft, commercial.

draft, bank

>A check drawn by one bank against funds deposited to its account in another bank.

draft, commercial

>A credit instrument which is initiated by the person who is to receive the money. The drawer sends it to the drawee who accepts it by writing his or her name across the face of the instrument.

draft, sight

>A draft that is payable on demand.

draft, time

>A draft that is to be paid at a future, specified date.

drawee

>Any party upon whom a draft is drawn and from whom the payment of the draft is expected. In normal business transaction, the drawee is usually the buyer of the goods.

drawer

>Any party who draws a draft or check upon another for the payment of funds. Also called the maker of the instrument.

drawing account

>An account set up in a single proprietorship or partnership in order that the owner or partners may make withdrawals. Also, an advance against future sales as a method of compensation to salespeople.

drop-shipper

>Also known as desk-jobber. A wholesaler who generally takes title to merchandise but does not warehouse it or stock it since the manufac-

turer ships directly to the retail customer against orders solicited by and sent in by the drop-shipper.

drum printer

An impact printer that prints line-by-line using a rotating steel cylinder imprinted with a wide variety of characters.

dual pricing

The selling of the same product in different markets at different prices.

due date

The date on which a note, draft, or other negotiable instrument is due and payable.

due presentment

When a note or bill is made payable on a specific future day, it must be presented to the drawee on that day and payment demanded. Presentment one day late results in the holder's losing all rights against the endorsers.

dummy director

A nominal director or one who acts for another on the board of directors of a corporation. Such a director votes as instructed by the real owner or powers behind a corporation.

dump

To transfer data en mass from one part of a computer system to another, or from one computer to another.

dumping

>The sale of excess production in a foreign market below the price for which the product is sold in the domestic market.

Dun & Bradstreet, Inc.

>A company involved in the gathering and distribution of business credit information.

duplex line

>A communications channel between two computers which allows both components to send and receive at the same time. See also full duplex.

duties, compound

>Tariffs which levy both specific and ad valorem taxes on the same products.

duties, specific

>Tariffs which are levied on individual commodities at so much per unit, or pound, or ton.

duty

>A tax imposed on the importation or exportation of goods.

E

EAP

See definition of employee assistance program.

earned surplus

The same as retained earnings. See definition of retained earnings.

earning power

The ability of a corporation to earn money on invested capital. The ratio of net earnings to capital stock.

earnings

The profits of a company after cost of goods sold and expenses are deducted from income.

earnings, retained

Profits of a company which are retained by a corporation as distinguished from those which are distributed as dividends.

easement

A right possessed by one person to use the real property of another for a specific purpose.

EBCDIC

>Acronym for extended binary coded decimal interchange code. The code used by IBM's large computers to convert alphanumeric information into digital form and vice-versa.

economic order quantity (EOQ)

>The least cost (minimum) quantity of materials or supplies which should be ordered to reflect the cost of carrying inventory. The EOQ is the quantity where the cost of ordering is equal to the cost of carrying the inventory over a period of time.

economic wealth

>Those goods and services which are scarce and valuable and therefore measured in terms of money.

economics

>The study of what we do with the resources we have at our disposal in order to get the most of what we want in the way of material benefits.

economy

>A way of getting a living. The system under which a group or class of people attain their living by whatever means they adopt, such as bartering, buying, plundering or parasiting.

EDP

>Abbreviation for electronic data processing. All computer-based activities are included in this term.

EEOC

>See Equal Employment Opportunity Commission.

elasticity of demand

> The change in demand for a good or service given a change in its price. Elasticity is determined by the percentage change in quantity bought divided by the percentage change in price.

electronic

> Using electricity as the means of accomplishing work, without converting it to another form. Examples would be computers, television and other media.

electronic funds transfer (EFT)

> This term refers to the use of computers in banking to automate banking functions such as deposits, withdrawals, transfers between accounts and the like.

electronic mail

> The sending and receiving of messages via computer or telecommunications.

electronic spreadsheet

> A computer software package ideally suited for financial planning, project management, inventory control, etc. because of its grid structure, versatility and ease of use.

electrotypes

> Sometimes called "electros." A printing impression made by pressing a special waxlike preparation into the original plate of zinc or copper. The impression is then dusted with graphite to make it an electrical conductor after which a negative impression identical with the original is made.

eligible paper

> The promissory notes, drafts, bills of exchange and banker's acceptances which member banks can discount with a federal reserve bank.

em

> A unit of measure in printing. The square of any size type.

eminent domain

> The power of a government to take private property from citizens in return for the payment of a fair price as determined by a court.

emolument

> Remuneration for services rendered.

employee

> A person who performs services for another for wages or salary.

employee assistance program (EAP)

> A plan designed to help employees with personal problems by offering aid and counseling. Some problems addressed by an EAP are alcoholism, drug addiction, compulsive gambling, and depression. The EAP might provide financial assistance, recommend a counselor or direct the employee to a rehabilitation center.

employee relations

> The various contacts between a company and its employees brought about by the following: (1) things which are inherent in the work relationship, and (2) things which go wrong and need to be corrected.

employee stock ownership plan (ESOP)

> A benefit program that uses company stock to provide deferred compensation to its employees. Different from a pension plan, this type of program is also an incentive plan, designed to give employees a feeling of participation in the management of the company.

employer

> A person or business firm which hires one or more persons who work for a wage or salary.

employment

> The act of engaging a person in a job, trade, business, occupation, or profession. Also, the state of being employed.

employment agency

> A firm engaged in the business of bringing together persons seeking jobs and employers seeking workers.

employment-at-will

> A concept meaning that where no contract exists, an employer may fire an employee at any time, with or without cause. This term has been used recently to refer to various wrongful discharge suits brought by employees against their former employers, challenging the employment-at-will concept.

emporium

> A place of trade, a market place, or a commercial center.

endorsement

An indication by signature that a check or negotiable instrument has been transferred, and a guarantee that previous signatures or endorsements are genuine.

endorsement, blank

The signing of a negotiable instrument by a person to whom it is payable.

endorsement, conditional

The signing of a negotiable instrument, making it payable after a particular event has taken place.

endorsement, qualified

A limiting clause appended to the signature on a negotiable instrument, freeing the signer from responsibility in the event that the debtor does not honor the instrument.

endorsement, restrictive

The signing of a negotiable instrument with some form of restriction over the signature such as the statement "for deposit only."

endorsement, special

The signing of a negotiable instrument with the specific person to whom the signer wishes it payable stated above the signature.

endorser, accomodation

A third party who affixes his or her signature to the back of a note for a personal loan. He differs from a co-signer in that he is not required to pay until after the maker has defaulted on his obligation.

endowment policy

> A plan of insurance providing for payment to a policyholder of a definite sum of money, the face amount of the policy after a specified number of years.

end product

> The finished product which goes to the ultimate consumer.

enterprise

> A business firm established and operating for a profit; a business venture or undertaking. See definition of business.

enterprise, free

> A system in which relative freedom is guaranteed to all who engage in any type of production or marketing activity, subject only to social conventions and legal restraints. The expression usually refers to an economic system rather than a private firm within the system.

enterprise, private

> A business venture or undertaking not publicly owned or controlled.

entrepreneur

> One who is willing to take a business chance, to assume risk of success or failure. One who for profit starts a new business, launches new products in an uncertain market, or assumes the task of industrial expansion.

E.O.M.

Abbreviation for "end of month," referring to the date of payment for some goods or services purchased.

Equal Employment Opportunity Commission (EEOC)

An agency created by the U.S. Civil Rights Act of 1964 whose purpose is to end discrimination in the workplace and to encourage fair hiring programs and practices in business.

equilibrium

The point of maximum profit in a business where marginal cost equals marginal revenue. Also, the point where total spending (consumption plus investment) equals total national income.

equipment

Fixed assets which are usually movable and accessories for larger fixed assets.

equity

The net value of property obtained by subtracting all loans and charges against the property from the total value. Also, the appliction of principles of justice to particular court cases where the law, by reason of its universality, is deficient.

equity capital

The amount or value of a property over and above the total liens and charges.

ergonomics

> The study of the workplace and how to make the work environment safer and more comfortable for employees.

escalator clause

> A clause in a labor-management contract calling for an adjustment in wages as the cost of living index goes up or down.

escape clause

> A provision in a contract that excuses a party from liability under certain conditions outlined in the contract. A maintenance of membership contract permits an employee to withdraw from a union within a stated period of time without losing his or her job.

escrow

> Property placed in the hands of a trustee for delivery to a third person after certain, specified conditions have been fulfilled.

ESOP

> See definition of employee stock ownership plan.

estoppel

> In law, this refers to the act of preventing.

ethics, business

> That branch of moral study which deals with the duties which a member of business owes to the public, to the court, and to business associates.

ethics, code of

A system of principles or rules guiding the conduct of persons in the same business or profession.

evaluation

An attempt to appraise performance or worth.

excess profits tax

An additional tax placed on those business profits considered to be in excess of a reasonable amount.

exchange

The barter or interchange of commodities. Also, the giving or receiving money of one country for that of another country. Also, an organization for trading in commodities or securities.

exchange, stock

A place of business where shares of stock are bought, sold, and exchanged.

exclusive selling agency

A method of business combination wherein two or more producers form a single agency to market their products. Any sales organization which sells an exclusive product.

ex-dividend

Literally the term means "without dividend." When a stock is sold after the books of a corporation have closed for a period, it is sold

execution

"without dividend"; that is, the purchaser has no right to the dividend of the preceeding period.

execution

The phase of computer operation when the program is actually being run or processed.

executive

A person engaged in management or administrative work involving forethought, planning and execution.

executive, chief

The top executive in a business organization. Also the head of a government such as the President of the United States.

executive, junior

A person who is of more recent entrance or of lower standing in management. A manager of a department.

executor, executrix (fem.)

A person named in a will to carry out its provisions.

expansion

The act of spreading out or of enlarging a business enterprise by developing new markets, by enlarging or building new facilities, by increasing the number of personnel or by other similar means of growth. The term also is used to describe a period when the trend of general business is upward.

expedite

>To clear away obstacles or to make a job easier to do by taking whatever steps are necessary to facilitate or to accelerate its progess.

expenditure

>A disbursement. A payment for a good or a service.

expense

>An outlay, cost or price which is charged against the revenue of a business.

expense, administrative

>The same as a general expense. See definition of expense, general.

expense, entertainment

>The cost of entertainment which is stated in an account and charged to a business as an expense.

expense, general

>Also known as administrative expense. A type of business operating expense which is incurred in the operation of a business apart from the sales effort. For example, the payroll for office personnel other than sales personnel is a general expense.

expense, operating

>In accounting, an operating expense is one which a business firm incurs in the normal operation of its affairs, such as the cost for salaries and wages, for advertising, for depreciation and for taxes. Operating

expenses are divided into selling and general expenses. These are defined elsewhere.

expense, selling

A type of business operating expense which is incurred as a result of sales activities.

expense account

An account set up to reimburse employees of a business for expenses incurred in the execution of certain affairs of the firm. A statement submitted by an employee for reimbursement of expenses incurred in the conduct of affairs of the business.

exporter

A wholesale merchant who sells goods to be shipped to a foreign market.

Export-Import Bank (Eximbank)

An independent U.S. banking agency formed in 1934 to promote foreign trade by extending loans to borrowers outside the U.S. with the stipulation that the money be spent in the U.S. and repaid in U.S. dollars.

express mail

Special service offered by the U.S. Postal Service as well as private carriers that provides fast—usually "next day"—postal service.

ex-rights

This expression refers to a security ehich is not entitled to rights. A company may offer stockholders the right to subscribe to new or additional issues at a discount from the current market price until a certain date. After the date, the stock is bought and sold without this right.

extended term insurance

An alternative to taking the cash surrender value of a life insurance policy in the event the policy lapses, providing term insurance for a stated number of years depending on attained age and the amount of cash which accumulated in the legal reserve.

extension agreement

A written authorization by creditors in a bankruptcy proceeding to postpone the due date of their bills in order that a business firm can try to improve its financial condition.

extractive industry

The kind of industry which concerns itself with the removal of raw materials or resources from their source, such as coal mining, oil and lumbering.

extrapolation

In statistics this term refers to the extension of a trend line beyond known data.

F

fabricating

Putting shape or form to materials such as fabricating a fender for an automobile. Also, the act of putting together standardized parts as is done, for example, in building a fabricated house.

face value

The value of a negotiable instrument as stated on the face of the document.

facsimile equipment

A device that transmits a replica of the original document via telecommunication lines. Copied documents can be graphic as well as alphanumeric in nature.

factor

An element that contributes to any given result. For example, people, materials and capital are factors of productions. Also, a factor is a business firm which retails short-term notes to investors. See definition of factoring company.

factoring

> Short-term financing through the device of selling accounts receivable to a financing agency.

factoring company

> A financial organization, found particularly in the textile field, which specializes in loans on accounts receivable.

fair employment practices

> Compliance by an employer with labor legislation regarding employer-employee relationships.

fair trade

> Federal and state laws enabling sellers for resale to control the price at which goods will be resold.

fair value

> The amount that a property will bring, or is worth, in the market as of a specific day.

Fannie Mae

> See Federal National Mortgage Association.

farmers' market

> The same as public market. See definition of public market.

FASB

Financial Accounting Standards Board, a group of accounting experts who determine accounting standards in the U.S.

featherbedding

A union practice of providing more workers than are necessary to perform a given task.

feature syndicate

An organization which distributes feature articles, photographs, cartoons, and the like to various news media which subscribe to the service.

Federal Home Loan Mortgage Corporation

A government sponsored private corporation which sells securities in the form of mortgage participation certificates and guaranteed mortgage certificates. "Freddie Mac" also promotes a secondary market for conventional home mortgages by purchasing said mortgages from lenders and packaging them for sale in the form of securities.

Federal National Mortgage Association

A private corporation regulated by the U.S. Department of Housing and Urban Development. "Fannie Mae" issues two kinds of securities: one, backed by a mortgage portfolio; the other, a long term certificate backed by the agency's ability to borrow from the Treasury.

Federal Reserve System

A system of banks, chartered and supervised by the United States Government, which acts as a source of credit and as a depository of reserves, and which performs other services for all national banks and many state banks.

fee

A compensation for services rendered by someone other than a direct employee of a business firm.

fee simple

The absolute ownership of real property, giving the owner and his heirs the unconditional right to hold, use and dispose of it.

fiber optic cable

Thin glass "wires" capable of transmitting large amounts of data at very high speeds.

fidelity bond

A form of insurance which protects an employer against loss due to the dishonesty of any employee who occupies a position of trust with jurisdiction over funds.

fiduciary

One who holds property for another such as a bank, trustee or guardian.

field

One item of data consisting of several consecutive characters.

field training

A method of training salesmen under actual selling conditions rather than through a formal sales-training course.

FIFO

>Abbreviation of the expression, "first in, first out." A method of pricing inventory in which materials flowing into production are priced as if they flow into production in the same chronological order as they are brought into inventory.

file

>A system by which papers, records or data are arranged according to date, subject, or alphabetical order in order to present ready and easy access to the information.

file, tickler

>A file used to remind a person of things he or she wants to know on certain dates of the month. A file used to jog the memory, such as the filing of vouchers by the dates on which they must be paid.

finance

>That part of a business operation which concerns itself with the management of monetary affairs, dealing in such matters as plans for long-term and short-term capital.

finance bill

>A bill of exchange, secured or otherwise, drawn by a banker in one country on a banker in another, the funds for the payment of which must be provided by the drawer at maturity.

financial management

>The function of seeing that funds are available in adequate amounts when needed. Also, the job of raising and providing money for capital assets as well as operating needs.

financial ratios

> Ratios, such as the ratios between current assets and current liabilities, based on financial information about a business and used for analysis and as a basis for management decisions.

financial statements

> Published data about the monetary affairs of a business, used for analysis, interpretation and decision-making.

financier

> A person skilled in the principles of handling private or public monetary affairs.

financing, short-term

> The securing of funds for a business firm for relatively short periods of time, usually less than a year.

financing, wholesale

> A plan of financing products sold to a middleman. In the financing of automobiles, for example, a dealer may pay 10 to 20 percent of the wholesale price, while the balance is paid to the manufacturer or distributor by a finance company which retains title.

financing plan, retail

> A plan whereby the ultimate purchaser of such a commodity as an automobile makes a down-payment in cash or in trade and, for the balance, executes a conditional sales contract which is paid off on a monthly installment plan.

fire sale

> Goods sold at a great discount due to water damage, fire or another emergency.

firefighting

> An expression meant to indicate a highly-busy office in which one crisis after another keeps occurring. Instead of having sufficient time to plan ahead for the future, the office personnel are too busy trying to cope with putting out each emergency, or "fire," that pops up.

firmware

> Hardware that has preprogrammed computer functions already built in. A bootstrap program is an example of a utility function that comes built into a system.

fiscal

> Pertaining to the public treasury. Also, having to do with financial matters in general.

fiscal agent

> A financial representative. The individual, bank, or trust company responsible for performing duties for a corporation, such as the disbursement of funds for payment of dividends, the redemption of bonds and coupons at maturity and the payment of rent.

fiscal policy

> The policy pursued by a government in connection with such matters as taxation, public debt, currency, public appropriations, and expenditures. Also, the financial policy pursued by a company.

fiscal year

One year of financial operation of a business or of a government. Any 12 months selected as an accounting period.

fixed benefits plan

A pension plan where the benefits are based on a fixed or inflexible percentage.

fixed capital

Economic goods such as plant, equipment, and other durable assets which will be used over a period of years.

fixed rate mortgage

A property loan whose interest rate remains constant throughout the life of the loan.

flat rate

This refers to a standard charge for a good or service, or per unit of a good or service. Also, a pay structure which offers a single rate of pay for each level.

fleet

A group of company owned vehicles used in the line of work, such as a sales fleet.

flexible benefits

A relatively new term, many corporations now offer their employees a choice of the kinds of benefits (e.g. medical, dental, life insurance, etc.)

they want. The employee makes his selection from the choices offered, and then has the cost of those benefit plans deducted from his paycheck. The company provides the benefits; the employee has the choice of which one he wants, if any.

flexitime

Also, flextime. A flexible work schedule which allows employees to make their own daily work schedule as long as it covers a prescribed period of time each day and totals a prescribed number of hours each week.

float

In banking, this term refers to checks which are in transit, that is checks which are in the process of being collected and converted to cash.

floater (floating policy)

An insurance policy which covers movable property, for example, jewelry or a fur coat, as opposed to the contents of a house which remain, for the most part, stationary.

floating interest

Interest rates which vary according to the general market interest rate.

floor

The area of a security exchange where actual trading occurs.

floppy disk

A flexible, thin plastic disk, coated with material which can absorb electromagnetic impulses, used for storing data.

flow diagram

> A diagram which shows the flow of work on the floor plan of a factory. It is used in factory planning before machinery and equipment are purchased.

flow of work

> The way that materials being processed pass through a plant, preferably in the shortest time at minimum cost.

flowchart

> A graphic representation of how information is processed within a specific program. A flowchart is very useful in planning program structure. See also data flow diagram.

F.O.B. destination

> Abbreviation for free-on-board. An agreement for paying freight whereby the vendor agrees to pay all freight charges.

F.O.B. shipping point

> Abbreviation for free-on-board. An agreement for paying freight whereby the vendor agrees to place merchandise free on board at the point from which it will be shipped. The purchaser is responsible for shipping charges from this point on.

focus group

> In marketing, a small but highly selective representative group of consumers will be asked for their views on a potential new product or service. Since the sample test group is selected at random, their views are considered as being a good indication of how the product or service will be received by the larger market in general.

font

> A particular style of typeface used by a printer. Examples are Courier, Elite, Gothic, Roman, Pica, etc.

footer

> The material below the text at the bottom of each page of a document, often just the page numbers but may include section numbers, chapter numbers, titles, etc. See also header.

forecasting

> The act of making an estimate of future business operations. The immediate or long-range prediction of future sales, production, prices, financial requirements, etc., for the purpose of planning ahead.

forecasting, sales

> The act of making an estimate of dollar or unit sales which will be made during a future period of time under a proposed marketing program or plan.

foreign exchange

> The methods whereby buyers and sellers in foreign trade pay and receive payment for goods.

foreman

> A member of management on one of the lower levels of supervision. A person above the level of a first-line supervisor and below the level of middle management. A person in charge of a group of workers at the workbench level.

forfeit

> To lose the right to something by some error, fault, offense, or crime.

forgery

> The alteration of a document or instrument with intent to defraud or to prejudice any individual.

form letter

> A standard letter, written on a subject of frequent recurrence, duplicated and sent to different persons without essential change other than addresses.

format

> To prepare a document for printing by aligning text, inserting paragraphs, numbering pages; usually done semi-automatically by a word processing program. Also, to prepare a disk to receive data. See also initialize.

formula investing

> The practice of buying and selling securities based on some predetermined course of action. For example, an investor may sell common stocks and buy preferred stocks when the market, on the average, rises above a certain point, and sell preferred stocks and buy common stocks when the market declines below that point.

FORTRAN

> Acronym for formula translation. A popular programming language used mainly on large computers and best suited for scientific or mathematical problems.

Fortune 500

An annual listing of the 500 largest U.S. corporations, published by Fortune magazine.

founders' shares

A portion of a corporation's capital stock, with special privileges or stipulations, issued to its promoters or founders for services rendered.

franchise

A privilege or right conferred by grant by a sovereign authority upon an individual or a business. The exclusive right granted to an individual to promote a product or service within a specified territory.

franchise fee

The fee charged by a city or state government to a corporation wishing to do business. This fee is in addition to the incorporation fee. It is a charge for permission to continue as a corporation.

fraud

A false representation of a fact made by one party with the intention that the other party act upon it, and which is relied on and acted on by the other party.

Freddie Mac

See definition of Federal Home Loan Mortgage Corporation.

free good

Any good such as air which is not scarce or is in such abundance that as much of it as wanted can be had without effort or cost.

frequency

> In statistics, this term refers to the number of cases found at each unit of measurement or at each class interval.

frequency distribution

> In statistics, this expression is used to describe the act of distributing any list of figures which are to be used in a computation into the number of times similar items appear. This is a necessary step prior to computing an average.

fringe benefit

> A supplement to wages received by workers, such as paid holidays, paid vacations, pensions, and insurance benefits.

frozen account

> An account which has been suspended in payment until a court order or legal process again makes it available for withdrawal.

full duplex line

> As distinguished from half duplex and simplex lines. See duplex line.

functional approach

> An approach to the study of anything from the point of view of what it does rather than what it is.

functional organization

> A type of organization setup which is based on specialists doing the work. Because of this specialization, there is no single line of authority

but rather multiple lines. Each employee is responsible to someone above him or her for each specific part of his or her work.

fundamental analysis

In investments, this expression refers to the evaluation of particular stocks and bonds by studying such factors as the financial status of the company, its competitive position, and general economic conditions. This kind of analysis differs from technical analysis which is defined elswhere.

funds

Sums of money or resources to be spent or used for specified purposes.

funds statement

In budgetary control this expression refers to a prepared report on the sources and application of funds for a given period of time in order to account for changes in working capital.

futures

Contracts for future delivery, such as a sale of wheat at an agreed-on price for delivery at a specified future date.

futures market

A speculative purchase or sales on the commodity exchange which calls for delivery at some future date. If it is a purchase, the buyer takes a "long" position; if it is a sale, the buyer takes a "short" position. These two terms are defined elsewhere.

G

gang boss

>A foreman or person in charge of a group of persons in a functional organization.

Gantt chart

>A graphic representation used as an aid to effective scheduling and control of various aspects of production by setting up graphically on a time scale when certain events in production are to take place, or where deadlines are to be met.

garnishment

>An order commanding a third party, such as an employer who owes wages to a worker, to pay a sum owed by the worker to his or her creditor.

gatefold advertisement

>An insert that unfolds to a size larger than the two-page size of the magazine into which it is inserted.

get the sack

>A slang term meaning to be fired or dismissed from one's job.

gilt-edge

> Securities of the highest quality as to lien protection and as to coverage of charges by earnings.

gimmick

> A device or stunt used in advertising or selling to motivate the prospect in the manner desired.

GNP

> See definition of Gross National Product.

going concern

> Any profit-making business that is actively operating as distinguished from one which has gone out of business.

going over one's head

> This slang expression refers to a subordinate bringing a problem to an upper level manager or supervisor due to dissatisfaction with his or her immediate supervisor's abilities or actions.

gold-bricking

> The use of excuses or devious means by an employee to shirk his or her duty.

golden handcuffs

> When an individual is obliged to remain at a job because financial benefits would be lost upon resignation.

golden handshake

> When an employee is dismissed from employment but also given a large cash bonus.

goldsmith's note

> A forerunner of the modern bank note. A goldsmith would give a written promise to pay on demand a stated sum to a customer or to a bearer. Thus, such a note was a demand promissory note.

gold standard

> A monetary system in which the unit of value is the value of a given quantity of gold in a free gold market.

goods

> In economics, the term means commodities and services. In marketing, it means commodities as distinguished from services.

goods, durable

> Also called hard goods. Items which have a relatively long life, a high price and a repossession value. Durable goods are distinguished from soft goods which are defined elsewhere.

goods, economic

> Wealth or scarce and valuable goods owned by man. Economic goods are the kind that are produced because man places a value on them as distinguished from free goods which are not produced because they are not scarce.

goods, finished

Economic goods which have been fully produced and are therefore ready to be sold to the public. Goods ready for consumption.

goods, free

Those things which are superabundant and are not subject to being owned as distinguished from economic goods which are scarce and are therefore valued.

goods, hard

The same as durable goods. See definition of goods, durable.

goods, insistence

The same as specialty goods. See definition of specialty goods.

goods, semifinished

Materials or components which have undergone certain manufacturing processes and which are in inventory until they are needed for assembly into finished products.

goods, soft

Merchandise such as clothing which normally has a short life and little repossession value, as distinguished from hard goods.

goods, unascertained

Goods which are either (1) not in existence at the time of the contract, or (2) mixed with other goods so that the particular goods to be delivered are still undetermined.

goodwill

>The disposition of a customer to return to the place where he or she has been well served. Many business firms carry goodwill as an asset in their accounting records.

gopher

>A slang term referring to an assistant who runs errands for others. It comes from the words "go for" as in "go for coffee" or "go for sandwiches," etc.

grace period

>A period after a debt or an insurance premium is due during which a debtor or insured can make payment without incurring a penalty or losing protection.

grandfather clause

>An exemption from a new statute based on previous circumstances. For example, a new law or policy requiring employees to take an examination before being hired would probably exempt those who are already hired.

grant

>A gift or transfer of funds or property.

graphic art production

>This term encompasses such arts as engraving, photography, paper, inks, silk-screen reproductions, binding, intaglio printing, planographic printing, relief printing, topography.

graphics display terminal

> A CRT that displays pictorial representations as well as alphanumeric characters.

greenmail

> A slang expression and variation of the word "blackmail." Greenmail is the payment by a company to an unwelcome investor for his stock in order to prevent a takeover of control. The term originated when payments exceeded the market price of the stock and thus gave unwelcome investors a preferential position relative to other stockholders because of the takeover threat.

grey collar worker

> An employee whose job entails duties that are both physical (blue collar) and administrative (white collar) in nature.

grievance

> A complaint about an injury, unjustice, or wrong, whether supposed or imaginary, brought to a company's attention by an employee.

grievance procedure

> The steps to be followed by a worker, and in some cases by management, in airing a complaint regarding such business problems as working conditions and wages.

gross margin

> An expression used in retailing to refer to the average over-all markup percentage on goods sold. The term is also used as synonymous with gross profit. See definition of gross profit.

Gross National Product (GNP)

    The nation's output of goods and services during the period of a year, expressed in dollar terms.

gross profit

    The result of subtracting cost of goods sold from the revenue or income received. This is called gross profit as distinguished from net profit, because other business expenses have not yet been deducted.

group banking

    A form of banking enterprise in which a group of investors form a holding company in order to acquire ownership or control of several banks.

growth stock

    A stock which appreciates in value, usually because the corporation is successful and is experiencing profitable expansion.

guarantee

    A pledge that a good or service will be replaced if it does not prove satisfactory. A positive assurance that a specified good or service will function properly or will be repaired or replaced.

guarantor

    A person who agrees to fulfill an obligation provided the individual who is responsible for discharging the obligation is unable to do so.

guaranty

>The act of agreeing to fulfill an obligation provided the individual who is responsible for discharging the obligation is unable to do so.

gypsy

>A term referring to a taxi or truck driver who owns and operates his or her own vehicle.

H

hacker

>A slang term referring to a computer hobbyist.

half-duplex

>A connection between two electronic components which allows only one of them to send or receive information at any time.

half-tone reproduction

>A technique used in printing to give the impression of shading in pictures by the use of dots produced by photographing the object behind a fine screen.

handbills

>A form of advertising which is distributed on the street or to the home of the prospective customer.

handbook, employee

>A manual designed to give an employee information one should know about policies related to one's job and one's work environment.

handicapped worker

    A worker with a physical disability.

hands on test

    The testing of a new machine, computer, system, etc. by putting it to actual use.

hard copy output

    A physical copy of computer output such as a paper printout, microfilm or microfiche, as distinguished from soft copy output such as that of a video display on a CRT.

hard disk

    A rigid hard computer disk, enclosed in a sealed container, which functions similarly to a floppy disk but can store much more information and access it faster.

hardware

    The physical components of a computer system as distinguished from the programming or software aspect.

hazard pay

    A wage differential paid to employees who perform unusually or extremely dangerous jobs.

head

    The electromechanical component of a disk drive which moves over the disk to store and retrieve information from it.

header

> The material above the text on each page of a document; often just the page number, but may include section number, chapter number, titles, etc. See footer.

headhunter

> A slang term referring to an executive search firm.

health benefits

> The health insurance provided by an organization for its employees in case of sickness, accident, or other health-related losses.

health maintenance organization (HMO)

> A membership health insurance plan that provides total health care by a group of physicians, affiliated with specific hospitals and clinics, all for a fixed monthly fee. In order to be covered by the plan, an individual must see one of the participating physicians. An HMO allows for preventative treatments, such as a yearly physical exam, as well as accident and sickness care.

hedging

> A transaction designed to eliminate or reduce the risk in another transaction. The act of selling against previous purchases or buying against previous sales in order to eliminate as far as possible either loss or gain due to price changes taking place from the time of the original transaction until the time when the materials, goods, or commodities are needed.

hidden asset

> An asset whose value is higher than that stated in the company's financial statements.

high-level language

A programming language typified by BASIC, which has many terms similar to human language and is relatively easy to learn.

histogram

A synonym for bar chart.

hit the bricks

A slang term meaning to go on strike.

hit the deck

A slang term meaning to go to work.

holder in due course

A person who, in the ordinary transaction of business, has possession of a negotiable instrument under the following conditions: (1) that it is complete, (2) that it is not overdue or, to one's knowledge, previously dishonored, (3) that it was taken in good faith and for value, and (4) that at the time it was negotiated there was no notice of any infirmity in the instrument or defect in the title.

holding company

A company that holds stock in other corporations. Usually a holding company is a nonoperating company in that it does not engage directly in operating activities such as production and marketing. See also definition of pyramiding.

Hollerith code

>The system used on a keypunch card to represent data. Named for Herman Hollerith who first developed the concept of the punched card in the late nineteenth century.

homeowner's policy

>A form of insurance which provides broad peril coverage for a private dwelling as well as comprehensive personal liability.

honor

>To pay a note, check, bill of exchange, or other negotiable instrument at maturity according to its conditions.

housekeeping

>In computer terms this refers to setting up the variables and constants in a program as a necessary step before any productive work can be performed by the computer.

human resources

>A term referring to the employees of an organization, or the members of a society.

human resources accounting

>A concept that employees of a company are valuable assets and should be accounted for in the same way as other capital assets.

human resources management (HRM)

A management strategy that views employees as integral parts of the organization, and whose objective is to obtain maximum participation and productivity from them.

hush money

A slang term for a bribe. Money given to buy one's silence.

hypothecate

To deposit property without giving up title or possession in order to secure a loan.

hypothecated account

In banking, this expression refers to an account such as a savings account or a trust account which a borrower pledges as collateral for a loan.

I

IC

Abbreviation for integrated circuit. Sometimes used as a synonym for chip. Consists of tiny electronic components, many thousands of which can be held on a chip.

impact

In advertising, impact means a forcible impression which a good advertisement makes on the audience at whom it is slanted.

impact printer

Any one of a number of devices that print computer output by striking an inked ribbon against a page. The impact causes the image to be printed.

import quotas

Designated amounts of specified commodities which a nation will allow to enter its borders in a given year.

importer

A wholesale merchant who buys goods from foreign business firms for domestic use.

impulse buying

The buying of merchandise at the time it is seen without any forethought or preplanning.

in kind

Also, payment in kind. Meaning to return or replace in a similar manner or with similar goods.

in the black

A slang term meaning to show a profit.

in the money

A slang term to describe a call option in which the strike price is below that of the market price of the stock.

in the red

A slang term meaning to show a loss.

in transit

Also, in transitu. Meaning, in the process of being shipped.

incentives

Inducements either financial or non-financial for performance above some standard or designated level.

income

The money return or other material benefits arising from the use of wealth or from the services of free, human beings. An increase of wealth or money resulting from interest on capital, payment for labor, and rent.

income statement

Also, statement of income. The statement of revenues and expenses for a company for a given period, resulting in a net profit or loss figure.

indirect labor

Labor not specifically identified with any work directly affecting the manufactured product.

individual retirement account (IRA)

A self-contributory pension plan. An individual can deposit up to $2000.00 of earned income in an IRA. This amount is fully tax deductible and interest earnings on the IRA are also tax exempt until withdrawal upon retirement.

indoctrination

A training program designed to give a new employee an understanding of the details of his or her job.

inducement

An incentive, argument, reason or fact used to persuade a person to take action, such as a reason given to buy a good or service.

induction

The process of bringing an accepted applicant into a business firm by reviewing with him all phases of the employment contract - duties, salary, hours of work, overtime arrangements, fringe benefits, and the like.

industrial democracy

An economic system in which industry has the right to choose what means of production it will use, and what product or products it will produce.

industrial distributor

A wholesaler who sells to factories or industrial buyers.

industrial fatigue

A weariness experienced by workers who have been engaged in work for too long a period of time. Such fatigue reduces a worker's perceptiveness and makes one prone to accidents.

industrial goods

Products sold to be used in the further processing of consumer goods.

industrial psychologist

A person who studies, writes, works or is versed in psychology as related to industry. A person concerned with problems such as providing pleasant working conditions for employees.

industrial relations

The relations which management experiences with groups of employees such as unions, as distinguished from personnel management which deals with employees as individuals. The term often refers to collective bargaining from the point of view of management.

Industrial Revolution

The period of rapid changes in economic organizations and technology which began in England in 1750 and in the United States about a century later. The period which saw production shift from the domestic stage to the factory system and from manual power to machine power.

industry

All non-agricultural and non-distributive business activity, including manufacturing, processing, and mining. A group of companies engaged in the same type of business activity.

industry, analytic

A type of industry in which the basic substance is broken down into a number of other materials which may or may not be similar to the basic substance. The petroleum refining industry is an example.

industry, assembly

The same as assembling. See definition of assembling.

industry, synthetic

A type of industry in which a number of different materials are combined to form a single product as in the manufacture of rayon.

infirmity

Any act or omission, in the creation or transfer of title, which would invalidate an instrument.

inflation

An increase in prices or a decrease in the value of money due to a shortage of goods or to an increase of money in circulation or or the upward pressures on prices because of the struggle for higher wages by labor which in turn stimulates management to push up prices.

information

>Data which has been organized so that it is meaningful and useful to people, as distinguished from raw data.

initialize

>To prepare a computer system, program or individual disk for use. See also format.

injunction

>A command of a court of equity ordering a defendant to refrain from doing or continuing to do an act injurious to the plaintiff's interest.

input

>The materials which combined make up a product ready for final consumption. Also, information or data for entry into a computer system.

input unit

>Any device, such as a disk or terminal, used to input data into a computer.

inquiry

>A request for information directed to a business, such as a request for an advertised booklet or for information about a product.

insert

>An enclosure in letters, pay envelopes, or packages which gives information about a product or a service.

insistence goods

The same as specialty goods. See definition of specialty goods.

insolvency clause

A clause in credit-insurance contracts providing that losses under the policy may be filed with the insurance company only if the customer becomes insolvent.

insolvent

Not being capable of meeting debts as they mature. Even though the total assets of a business might exceed liabilities, a business could be insolvent if the assets could not be converted into sufficient cash to meet current obligations as they mature.

inspection

The act of measuring the extent to which standards have been observed in a manufacturing process and of eliminating or rejecting any part of the product not up to standard.

installment buying

A means of buying whereby the buyer agrees to make payments at specific intervals in the future for goods received at the time of the purchase.

installment plan

A system of credit whereby a consumer receives immediate possession and use of articles purchased in return for a down-payment and a promise to pay the balance owed in a series of payments.

installment selling

> A method of selling in which the seller keeps title to the goods until the buyer makes the last of a series of payments at specified intervals after the purchase.

institutional approach

> An approach to marketing which studies the institutions which perform the various functions of marketing. Other approaches are the commodity approach and the functional approach which are defined elsewhere.

institutional investor

> A company, such as a pension fund, mutual fund or bank, that invests large sums in securities.

instrument

> A written document in which some right is conferred or some contractual relationship is expressed.

insurable interest

> A pecuniary interest in property or life which an applicant must have in order to obtain insurance protection.

insurance

> A contract between an insurance company and an insured which binds the company, in return for the payment of a premium, for losses described by the contract.

insurance, accident and sickness

> A form of health insurance which pays a weekly income to the insured if he or she cannot work due to sickness or accident.

insurance, accidental death and dismemberment

> A form of insurance which provides protection for accidental loss of life, limbs or sight.

insurance, accounts receivable

> A form of insurance which gives protection for loss of accounts receivable resulting from destruction or disappearance of records.

insurance, broad form personal theft

> Insurance coverage for loss by theft and mysterious disappearance of property from the premises, and for loss of property placed for safekeeping with a bank, trust, safe deposit company, warehouse, or occupied dwelling.

insurance, builder's risk

> A form of insurance which provides protection for the builder during the course of construction.

insurance, cargo

> A form of marine insurance which provides protection against loss of cargo.

insurance, casualty

A form of insurance protecting against claims arising from unfortunate accidents or occurrences other than fire, transportation of goods, and death. The common types are automobile, theft, accident, health, public liability, aviation, and workmen's compensation.

insurance, collision

A form of car insurance which indemnifies for damage to the insured's automobile as a result of impact.

insurance, credit

A form of insurance which gives protection to the accounts-receivable asset of a business by assuming the risk of above normal credit losses. Also, a form of life insurance in which a creditor is beneficiary of a policy equal to the amount of the debt.

insurance, endowment

A life insurance contract which provides for payment of the amount of the insurance to the beneficiary in the event of the insured's death during the policy period, or to the insured himself if he survives to the end of the period.

insurance, fire

A form of property insurance whereby the insured is protected against loss to his property because of fire or related causes.

insurance, freight

A form of marine insurance which provides protection for loss of freight earnings or for loss of cargo.

insurance, group

>Various forms of life and health insurance sold in a master contract to a business firm with certificates issued to employees covered. Group plans usually cover groups of 25 or more employees and are offered regardless of the physical condition or age of applicants.

insurance, hospitalization

>A form of insurance which pays room and board benefits and hospital extras to an insured and, in most cases, to the insured's dependents.

insurance, hull

>A form of marine insurance providing protection against loss occuring because of damage to the hull of a ship.

insurance, industrial

>A form of life insurance which is sold in policies of small amounts, the premiums for which are usually collected by an agent on a weekly basis.

insurance, inland marine

>A form of marine insurance providing a wide range of protections, including the following: (1) transportation floater, (2) parcel-post policy, (3) salespeople's floater, (4) jewelers' block policy, (5) personal-property floater and (6) manufacturers' output floater. These forms of protection are defined elsewhere.

insurance, key-man

>A form of insurance taken out on the life of a key person in a business situation in order to protect the business or individuals against the loss they would experience should the key person die.

insurance, liability

> A form of insurance which protects a person against claims made by the public for real or fancied injuries while using the facilities or products of the insured.

insurance, life

> A form of insurance in which a stipulated sum is paid to a beneficiary upon the death of the insured or, in some plans, to the insured upon reaching a specified age.

insurance, limited payment life

> A form of insurance which requires the insured to pay an annual premium for a definite number of years in return for which the carrier will pay the face amount of the policy to a beneficiary upon the death of the insured.

insurance, marine

> A form of insurance which protects against various hazards of trade on the waters of the earth.

insurance, mercantile open-stock burglary

> A form of insurance which protects against merchandise losses resulting from the forcible entry of burglars after the premises have been closed.

insurance, money and securities — broad form

> A form of insurance which protects against the loss of money and securities because of robbery. The broad form provides protection for (1) all loss of money and securities, (2) loss due to robbery of merchandise, and (3) loss due to burglary of merchandise from safes.

insurance, ordinary life

> A form of insurance which requires the insured to pay an annual premium during his life in return for which the carrier pays the face amount of the policy when the insured dies.

insurance, products liability

> A form of public liability insurance which provides protection to a businessperson should his or her product cause damages or injuries to someone.

insurance, property damage

> A form of car insurance which pays damage to another car or to property not belonging to the insured up to the amount of the policy.

insurance, term

> A form of insurance in which the carrier in return for premium paid promises to pay a stipulated sum of money upon the death of the insured, provided the death occurs within a predetermined period.

insurance, unemployment

> A form of insurance, usually handled by the state, which pays benefits during a fixed period of time to persons unemployed.

insurance, workers' compensation

> A form of insurance which protects an employer by paying an employee for loss of income and for medical expenses incurred if the sickness was caused by the work environment or if the injuries were received while the employee was working.

insurance policy

> A written contract spelling out the essential details of an insurance risk assumed by an insurance company for a person or business.

intaglio printing

> A form of printing in which the surface of the plate to be duplicated is depressed and the paper on which the duplication is made is forced into this depression.

intelligent terminal

> A computer terminal which has programming and computing capabilities as distinguished from a dumb terminal.

interactive

> A computer system which allows the user to enter and change programming and data more or less simultaneously.

interchange reports

> Credit information which is disseminated from a central bureau after having been gathered from many local bureaus which have pooled their knowledge about the business or individual.

interest

> Money paid for the use of money. The price or percent rate paid for the use of borrowed money.

interest, accrued

> Interest that has accumulated but has not been paid or collected.

interest, compound

> The price or percent rate paid on both the principal lent and on the unpaid interest.

interest, effective rate of

> The actual percentage of interest paid on a loan as distinguished from the stated percentage which appears on the contract.

interest, nominal rate of

> The amount or percentage of interest which is stated on a contract or note as distinguished from the effective rate of interest which may be considerably more.

interest, simple

> The price or percent rate paid only on the principal lent as distinguished from compound interest which pays a price for the unpaid interest as well.

interface

> Any connection between components of a computer system, or of different computer systems.

interlocking directorate

> This expression refers to a condition which exists when one person serves two or more companies as a director. By law this is forbidden if the companies are natural competitors, have combined capital, surplus and undivided profits of $1,000,000 or more and are engaged in interstate commerce.

internal audit

> An audit of company operations carried out by an employee of the company rather than an outside agency. A typical internal audit will check all aspects of operations as well as a complete check of finance and accounting procedures.

internal rate of return (IRR)

> A method of evaluating and ranking risky investments, using time discounted cash flows and the opportunity cost of capital.

interpolation

> In statistics this term refers to the estimation of points between known data.

interpreter

> A computer program which converts a program that a user has written in a high-level language into the given computer's machine language as the computer is running.

interstate commerce

> The manufacture, exchange, buying or selling of goods and services which takes place over state lines or among states.

interview

> The act of questioning or conversing in order to get information, to become acquainted, and the like.

interview, depth

> A personal interview, particularly in market research, in which the respondent cooperates fully in answering seemingly unrelated but

detailed questions, the answers to which will establish a pattern of motivation as well as of fact.

interview, exit

An interview with an employee prior to his or her separation from work with the organization.

interview, panel

A series of interviews used in market research in which a selected group of respondents are questioned a number of times in order to discover any changes in the opnions or knowledge of the respondents. The same question or questions are asked of the group each time.

interview, preliminary

The first interview which an employment officer has with an applicant.

interview, selection

An interview with a successful applicant who is to be notified he or she has received a job, or an interview with an employee who is being transferred to another job.

interviewing, jury system

A system of interviewing in which more than one executive interviews an applicant for a job.

intestate

A term referring to a deceased person who died without leaving a will.

intransitu

Goods in the act of being shipped.

intrinsic reward

A reward obtained from the job itself such as personal satisfaction, positive feedback, a sense of achievement, and the like.

inventory

All of a business' materials and supplies which are in storage, in process, or ready for sale.

inventory float

The rate of use of inventory in a plant.

inventory turnover

The number of times that a stock of goods has been replaced within a given period. Turnover is determined by dividing the number of units sold by the average units on hand.

investment banking

A form of business in which a financial institution buys stock and bond issues from corporations and distributes them, raising money for the company as well as itself.

investment company

The same as an investment trust. See definition of investment trust.

investment house

> A bank which aids corporations in raising long-term capital by selling and by underwriting corporate securities such as stocks and bonds.

investment tax credit

> A deduction from income of a percentage of the purchase price of a major fixed asset. Designed to encourage investment in plant and equipment for future growth and expansion.

investment trust

> Also called an investment company or a mutual fund. A company which uses its capital to invest in other companies. An open-end investment trust, often called a mutual fund, does not list its shares and buys them back when investors wish to sell out. A closed-end investment trust sells shares which are then bought and sold like any other stocks.

investor

> A person who invests in a business for the purpose of gaining income or profit.

invoice

> An itemized list of goods, stating their price and quantities sold, sent by the seller to the buyer.

I.O.U.

> Abbreviation of "I owe you." An admission that a debt is owed, but not a promise to pay it.

IRA

> See definition of individual retirement account.

IRR

> See definition of internal rate of return.

issue price

> The price at which a new issue of securities is placed on sale by the underwriters or agency handling the marketing of the securities.

J

jewelers' block policy

> A form of inland marine insurance which provides protection for stock of a jewelry business at the place of business as well as outside the premises. Coverage also includes jewelry property sent by registered mail, or by insured express, or during the time it is being delivered.

job, key

> The same as a benchmark job. See definition of benchmark jobs.

job analysis

> The process of determining the duties, responsibilities, authorities, relationships, and environment of a job.

job cost system

> The system where cost elements for each order worked on in the plant (or department) are collected separately.

job cycle

> A complete unit of work. In time study this refers to the motions with which a worker performs from the time he or she starts a unit of work until it is completed.

job description

>A written analysis of all of the pertinent facts relative to a specific duty or unit of work. A job analysis put in writing. See definition of job analysis.

job evaluation

>The process of making a systematic study of the relationship between all job values in a company. The comparing of the value of one job with that of all other jobs in an organization.

job hopping

>When a person holds many different jobs in a short period of time, he or she is known as a job hopper. Many firms are reluctant to hire job hoppers for fear that they will quit as soon as they are trained, thus wasting the company's time and money.

job lot

>A mixed assortment of goods that a merchant is willing to sell for a reduced price.

job security

>Job protection for an employee usually negotiated as part of a union contract.

job sharing

>When two persons, each working part time, perform a full time job.

job shop

>A company which contracts to perform work to customer designs. A company which makes products to order as distinguished from one which makes standard products.

job specifications

A description of the duties of a job, plus a description of the mental and physical qualifications, such as experience and skill, which are required of a person to fill it.

jobber

The same, in most trades, as wholesaler or wholesale merchant. A middleman who is engaged in the business of buying and selling merchandise.

joint account

A bank account owned by two or more people and subject to withdrawal by any of the owners' signatures.

joint liability

Also, joint and several liability. In law this means an obligation incurred by two or more parties both individually and together. The implication is that either all the parties are mutually responsible for the liability or any one party can be held individually responsible.

joint stock company

The forerunner of the modern corporation. A type of business organization in which a group of individuals organizes and receives shares for capital invested. As in a partnership each owner assumes unlimited liability, but as in a corporation, the shares are transferable.

joint tenants

The ownership by two or more persons of a share or an interest in real estate with the right of survivorship.

joint venture

A business undertaking by two or more persons who contribute capital to a single project. This differs from a partnership in that the element of any continuity is lacking.

journal

In accounting, this term refers to a book of original entry in which is maintained a chronological history of transactions of a business firm.

journal, cash disbursements

The same as check register. See definition of check register.

journeyman

A worker who has learned a handicraft or trade, as distinguished from an apprentice who is still in the process of learning.

joystick

A small device resembling the manual shift of an automobile, used for controlling certain computer programs, usually games.

judgment creditor

A person who has obtained a judgment against his debtor and can enforce execution.

judgment debtor

A person in debt against whom a creditor has obtained a judgment.

junk mail

A slang term referring to unsolicited direct mail advertisements which arrive in the mail.

K

K

A "digital thousand," or 1024 bytes.

Keogh plan

A contributory pension plan for self-employed persons that is similar to an IRA in that the funds deposited are tax deductible, and interest earned on the account is tax exempt until withdrawal at retirement. It differs from an IRA in that contributions can be much higher—up to 15 percent of earned income (but not exceeding $15,000.00) annually.

key account

The acount that is the most important client that a company services. Many times, a key account will be responsible for as much as 80% of a firm's business, although most firms try to balance out their accounts to more than just one key client.

keypunch

A machine which takes input from a keyboard and punches holes in paper cards which are then used by a card reader to provide input to a computer. This system of input, once widely used, has largely been replaced by disk drives.

kickback

A return, due to coercion or a secret agreement, of part of the money received by a person as wages, commissions, or fees.

kicked upstairs

A slang term referring to the removal of an individual whose performance was less than satisfactory, to a higher position in the company.

kiting

A way that depositors can force loans from banks in different locations by simultaneously cashing each other's checks and, at the same time, withdrawing the money deposited in their own checking accounts. This is a malpractice taking advantage of the time element involved in check collection by banks.

L

labeling, descriptive

A method of distinguishing between packaged goods by means of written descriptions on the labels affixed to the packages.

labeling, grade

A method of categorizing packaged goods according to levels of quality, weight and size by means of symbols which are written on labels affixed to the packages.

labels

Any markings, tags, or classifications placed on articles in order to identify them or to designate their ownership, price, quality or destination.

labor force

People who are 16 years of age and over, classified as employed or employable.

labor movement

The activities of workers when combined in concerted efforts to promote their interest. This collective movement, which was marked by the beginning of unions, has strengthened labor's ability to bargain with employers.

labor organization

A union composed of workers who band together in order to improve their economic welfare by presenting a united front in bargaining with management for such benefits as higher wages, shorter hours, better working conditions and greater security.

labor problems

Those difficulties which are caused by differences of opinion and of aims between management and labor.

labor relations

Management's relationships with individual workers, groups of workers, and unions.

labor turnover

Defined under the term turnover. See definition of turnover.

labor union

The same as labor organization. See definition of labor organization.

laissez-faire

The condition which exists in an economic system or an industry when the government does not interfere with competitive business methods. A philosophy which adheres to the principle that the government should not meddle in affairs of business.

LAN

    Acronym for local area network. See network.

landlord

    The owner of rented property such as land, apartments, buildings, hotels, and inns.

lapse

    In insurance, this terms refers to the discontinuance of insurance protection because the policyholder has failed to pay the premium before the expiration of the grace preiod.

laser printer

    A device that prints via a narrow beam of electromagnetic energy.

layoff

    The act of shutting down or curtailing the activities of a plant or business. The act of terminating the employment of workers.

layout

    An outlined diagram of what is to be accomplished. The components of an advertisement with pictures, headings, copy, signature, and other details arranged in the planned order of the finished advertisement.

layout, art

    The arrangement of pictures and illustrations in commercial art in order to attract attention, create desire and elicit action on the part of potential customers.

layout, plant

    An outlined diagram of the interior components of a manufacturing plant.

lead

    The name, address, and other pertinent information about a sales prospect.

lead report

    A summary of "leads" sent to salespersons or prepared by salespersons, containing such information as the name and address of the prospect, the medium producing the lead and the result of the sales presentation.

lead time

    In production, this refers to the amount of time taken between the completion of operations planning and the beginning of production. In inventory, lead time refers to the amount of time taken between placing and receiving an order.

lease

    A contract in return for rental payments, granting possession of specified property for the life of the party to whom the property is conveyed or for a period specified in the contract.

leasehold

    Referring to buildings or property under lease, such as leasehold agreements, leasehold improvements, and the like.

leasing asset

    An asset which is rented rather than owned by a business.

leave of absence

    A temporary departure from work granted by an employer for such reasons as illness, military duty, jury duty, or union business.

ledger

    A book of accounts. The final summary of debits and credits in various business accounts.

ledger, stock

    A ledger containing information about a corporation's capital in authorized shares.

legacy

    The same as bequest. See definition of bequest.

legal entity

    A being such as an individual, partner or corporation which, in the eyes of the law, has the right to make a contract and to be held responsible for acts.

legal personality

    A being created by law such as a corporation. See definition of corporation.

legal tender

    Any money recognized by law as being lawful for a debtor to use in paying a creditor. The creditor must accept legal tender in discharge of a debt unless the contract specifically states the type of money to be used.

lending institution

>A business whose prime purpose is to lend money on a borrower's promise to repay the principal sum borrowed plus a stated rate of interest.

lessee

>The person to whom the possession of specified property has been conveyed for a period of time in return for rental payments.

lessor

>The person who conveys specified property to another for a period of time in return for the receipt of rent.

letter of credit

>An instrument or letter issued by a bank, agreeing to accept drafts to be charged against the established credit of an individual or a business.

letter of credit, commercial

>The same as letter of credit. See definition of letter of credit.

letter of credit, traveler's

>A bank letter granting credit to a traveler and addressed to the bank's correspondents abroad.

letter quality printer

>This term is used to describe any of the impact printers whose printed output closely resembles that of a typewritten page.

letterpress printing

> The type of printing which is done by duplicating from type which is raised above the surface of the plate to be impressed.

leverage

> Also called trading-on-the-equity. The use of borrowed money in the expectation that the interest rate will be lower than the earnings which can be made on the money.

leverage, financial

> The ratio of total liabilities to total assets.

liabilities, current

> The debts of a corporation which are due and payable within the near future, usually a maximum of one year.

liability

> The claims of creditors and owners against the assets of a business.

liability, double

> Liability that is twice as much as invested capital of the stockholder. Bank stockholders at one time had to assume double liability for their investment.

liability, limited

> Liability which is limited to a stated amount. A shareholder of a corporation enjoys a limited liability because, in general, one cannot

lose more than one's capital investment in the company. Property owned outside the corporation is not jeopardized unless criminal action is involved.

liability, unlimited

A situation such as exists in a sole proprietorship wherein a person's wealth beyond the amount invested in the business is legally available in order to satisfy the claims of creditors.

licensing

A tax placed on a producer or seller for the right to conduct business affairs.

lien

A claim upon real or personal property to pay a debt or duty.

lien, carrier's

When the shipper ships the goods "collect," the carrier has a claim on the goods for the freight or express charges. This is a possessory claim, which means the carrier can retain possession of the goods as security for the charges due.

lien, common law

A claim based on common law. Also, a claim which arises from implication of the law rather one which is created by agreement of the parties.

lien, mechanic's

The legal enforceable claim which a person who has performed work or provided materials is permitted to make against title to the property or as a preferential person in the event the estate or business is liquidated.

LIFO

Abbreviation of the expression "last in first out." A method of pricing inventory by which materials flowing into inventory are priced as if they flow into production on the basis that the last materials bought are the first going into the production process.

light pen

A device used with a CRT terminal to actually "write" on the display screen in order to change data.

limited

Also known by the abbreviation "Ltd." A legal entity, similar to the U.S. corporation, created by the British or Canadian government. The word came from the concept of limited liability.

limited partnership

A form of business partnership in which one or more of the partners assume liabilities which are limited as distinguished from the principal partner or partners who assume unlimited liabilities.

line and staff organization

A combination of a line organization and a functional organization. Like the line organization this form provides that authority and responsibility be delegated from the top down. Like the staff organization, it sets up specialists to handle certain problems.

line cut

A method of printing by which a drawing is photographed on a piece of copper or zinc treated with a light sensitive chemical. The metal is then placed in acid which eats down the surface of the plate around the line-drawn image. The image is left standing in relief providing the printing face for the transfer.

line-haul service

The service provided by a railroad of transporting from one terminal to another as distinguished from switching and terminal services which may be performed by another company and which are solely within a terminal area.

line organization

An organizational structure in which employees within a department are responsible to one boss only and each department manager is responsible to one person only.

line printer

An impact printing device that prints information one line at a time as distinguished from serial or page printers.

lines of authority

The various ways that authority over areas of responsibility is spread down through an organization from top management to the workbench level.

linotype

> A typesetting machine which responds to the operator's touch by casting type in solid slugs.

liquid assets

> Coins, bank notes, and securities which can be converted instantly into cash.

liquid capital

> Known also as quick, current or fluid capital. Cash or assets which can be converted easily into cash.

liquidate

> To settle the affairs of a business and to cause it to cease to exist as a going concern.

liquidating dividends

> A return of capital to shareholders of a corporation.

liquidity

> A term used to refer to the degree which a corporation can meet its current liabilities with cash payments.

list price

> The stated price of a commodity or service before any discounts or allowances.

list selection

> In direct marketing, the choosing of lists of names, compiled according to certain characteristics, in order to target them for promoting a product or service.

lithography

> Literally means "writing on stone." A method of printing on a flat surfaced plate in which ink containing oil is transferred to paper. Wet parts of the plate not covered by the design receive no ink because the water repels the oil.

"live" program

> A radio or television program given by actual performers at the time of the broadcast.

load

> A term used in selling such things as securities, referring to the marketing costs of making a purchase. For example, the load for a share of stock is the sales commission and other costs of distribution.

load ahead schedule

> A written plan indicating the amount of production which has already been scheduled for a factory.

loan

> A transaction between two parties in which one party rents funds to a second party.

loan, broker's time

> A loan which is borrowed for a specific period of time by a broker who is able to estimate his minimum requirements for considerable time ahead and who wants to escape the uncertainty and trouble of renewing a call loan.

loan, call

> A loan which can be called in for payment any time the lending agency desires.

loan, consumption

> A loan to a person who uses the money to purchase a good or service meant for final consumption, such as a loan for an automobile bought for personal use.

loan, downstream

> The borrowing of money by a holding company and making such money available to subsidiary operating companies which could not obtain funds at such a favorable rate of interest.

loan shark

> An unscrupulous lender who charges exorbitant rates of interest and who may be more interested in taking over the collateral than in being repaid.

loaned servant

> An employee who is working temporarily for an employer other than his or her own.

locked-in

> This refers to a situation in which an investor does not sell securities because the profits realized would be subject to a high capital gains tax.

lockout

> An employer's refusal to permit workers to enter a plant to go to work.

log on

> To connect to a larger computer system and identify yourself as a valid user.

long

> A term used in investments to refer to the position of a security investor who has bought securities and is holding them in the expectation that the stock prices will rise.

long-term financing

> The methods of raising funds in a business firm which involve both investments made by owners and funds borrowed for several years, usually ten or more.

loop

> Part of a program which repeats itself, often by going back to previous lines when necessary.

loss leader

> The sale of an article below cost by a retailer as a means of attracting store traffic in the expectation that such traffic will lead to other purchases.

lot, carload

A railroad car full of goods. The rates for goods shipped in this manner are generally 15 to 30 percent lower than those for less than a carload lot.

lot, less than carload

Goods shipped by rail in quantities less than a full carload. (L.C.L.) The rates for less than a carload lot are considerably higher - 15 to 30 percent - than for goods shipped by carload.

lump sum payment

The payment in full of the face amount of an insurance policy rather than payment on the basis of some gradual payout plan.

luxury trade

Commerce in goods having a high value relative to their bulk. Costly goods which please the senses and are difficult to obtain.

M

machine, addressograph

    A machine used for addressing mail. It prints each address separately from characters embossed on a plate.

machine, punch card

    A machine which transfers information from an original document to a card by punching holes in predetermined positions.

machine language

    The most fundamental language of any computer, composed of binary digits—0's and 1's—which the computer itself uses to process data. All other languages must be translated into machine language before the computer can execute any instructions written in them.

magnetic core storage

    A method of storing information in computers in donut-shaped rings of ferro-magnetic material. Current is passed through the center of the ring to magnetize the magnetic core memory element.

magnetic disk storage

    A method of storing information in a computer by recording it on disks similar to a standard phonograph record. Information is read into or out of the disks by means of an arm which is able to enter into the stack of records and read from or write on either side of the disk. The recording process is one involving magnetic spots instead of physical grooves.

magnetic drum storage

A method of storing information in a computer that is faster than a magnetic core. Information is written on or read from magnetic spots on a rotating drum in the same manner that a tape recorder records and plays back.

magnetic storage

Any computer tape or disk used to store and retrieve information by varying electromagnetic charges on a coating which is usually made with some form of iron oxide.

magnetic tape input

A method of communicating with a computer through information which is recorded on a plastic recording tape. The information is coded as magnetic marks on the tape.

mailing list

A list of prospects maintained by a business to be used in direct-mail campaigns and in sales-promotion work.

mail order

Any order for goods which is received, filled, and returned by mail.

mail-order house

A wholesale or retail establishment which receives its orders and makes its sales by mail.

mainframe

> The largest type of computer system in terms of memory, programming and processing capability. Used in larger organizations where centralized or distributed data processing systems are in effect, and where remote terminals must "share time" on a central facility.

maintenance

> The upkeep of property, machinery, or equipment

maintenance, plant

> The care and supervising of repairs, heat, light, power, ventilation, operating of machinery, elevators, and workrooms in a plant or factory.

major medical insurance

> Health insurance that protects against large scale losses such as prolonged illness or serious accident, and pays for a percentage of the costs incurred beyond the deductible.

maker

> The signer of a promissory note and eventually the one who pays it.

management

> The collective body of those who direct any enterprise or interest. The judicious use or skilled application of people to accomplish an objective.

management, absentee

> The control and direction of a business by top executives who are separated from the operating divisions of the company. For example,

the home offices where the top executives work may be located in one city and the operating divisions may be located elsewhere.

management, administrative

The same as top management. See definition of top management.

management, centralized

A plan of control which concentrates most of the important middle management functions and decisions in one location. For example, buying, advertising, promotion and accounting for all locations of a firm may be done from its main office.

management, decentralized

A plan of control which allows a high degree of independence among branch offices or operating divisions in so far as middle management functions and decisions are concerned. For example, buying advertising and accounting may be performed by each branch office.

management, intermediate

Divisional executives. Sometimes called middle management. The level of management at which policies formulated by top management are communicated to the people who will actually carry them out.

management, middle

Also called intermediate management. Executives who are between top management and operating management. For example, department heads, branch managers, plant managers and production superintendents are classed as middle managers.

management, operating

Executives whose primary job is the supervision of workers. For example, plant supervisors and foremen are classed as operating managers.

management, personnel

The planning, directing and coordinating of activities concerned with securing, training, organizing and using employees.

management, sales

The directing of a business organization's distribution of products including such functions as hiring, training and controlling salesmen and establishing sales territories and quotas.

management audit

A system of evaluating an organization's administrative functions, including an appraisal and analysis of management's overall efficency and effectiveness in accomplishing corporate goals.

management by exception

A management technique by which executives focus on deviations from normal daily activities as opposed to taking an active role in all daily decision-making.

management by objectives (MBO)

A management technique by which both managers and subordinates devise a plan of action and goals to be accomplished over a period of time, with periodic appraisals to measure progress.

management by walking around (MBWA)

    The art of keeping one's staff happy and motivated by having the departmental manager walk around and talk to the individual employees in the office or in the factory. Theoretically, MBWA stimulates more communication between management and the workers.

management consultant

    A person hired by an organization to investigate and make recommendations on actions which should be taken in a particular area of business affairs.

management control

    That segment of management activities which concerns itself with seeing that results conform with plans. It involves establishing standards, delegating responsibility, taking corrective action, and assessing results.

management functions

    The work performed by executives such as planning, organizing, actuating and controlling.

management specialization

    The distribution of the work of management among experts in particular fields of activities in order to increase productivity, quality of performance, and accuracy.

manager

    A person charged with the responsibility of operating profitably a business enterprise or a segment of it. An individual granted the power to plan, organize, and control.

man-hour

> A unit of work performed by one person in one hour, especially used as a basis for wages and cost finding.

manifest

> The inventory of a ship's cargo, including the value, origin, and destination of each item.

manpower

> The aggregate of people in a locality or a nation who are either working or available for work.

manual, budget

> A specific and clear statement in writing of company policies and procedures in connection with preparation and use of the budget.

manual, organization

> A statement in writing which defines the duties and functions of the several departments, units, or individual positions in an organization, showing the relationship of one to another.

manual, policy

> A handbook issued to employees by a business firm, containing guiding principles to be followed in carrying out the affairs of the business.

manual, procedure

> A compilation of routines for handling various administrative operations, providing a new worker with a source of reference about his or her job.

manufacturer's agent

> A person who operates on an extended contractual basis with a manufacturer, selling within an exclusive territory, often handling noncompeting but related items, and having limited authority with regard to price and terms of sale.

manufacturers' output floater

> A form of insurance protection for a manufacturer, providing coverage on an "all risk" basis for property other than that located on the premises.

manufacturers' representative

> A sales specialist representing several manufacturers and selling a line of related products to specific customers (defined either geographically, or by industry, etc.)

manufacturing

> Producing goods, especially on a large scale, with the use of labor and of machines.

margin

> Markup as a percentage of selling price. Also, the money or security deposited with a broker by a client who is buying securities on credit. Also, the amount of equity a person has in securities after his or her purchase.

margin call

> A term used in investments to refer to a demand by a broker that a customer put up money or securities at the time a security is purchased on credit or when the margin account of the customer declines below a minimum set by the exchange or by the brokerage firm.

marginal productivity

> The amount that one additional increment of a variable factor of production will increase total production. For example, the marginal physical productivity of labor is the amount by which the addition of one laborer increases total output.

marginal revenue

> The amount which the sale of one additional unit of output adds to total revenue.

marginal trading

> Also called buying on margin. The purchasing of securities paid for in part by borrowing with the securities themselves used as collateral.

marginal utility

> The usefulness of an additional unit. A principle in economics which assumes that the acquisition of successive units has less want-satisfying power.

margin-of-safety

> An allowance over and above what is considered to be necessary to cover unforeseen emergencies.

markdown

> A reduction in the original selling price due to such reasons as overbuying, poor selection, shopworn goods, unpopular colors, or weak sales effort.

market

> The buying public for a product or service. An aggregate composed of prospective buyers and sellers, bringing to focus the conditions and forces which determine price (supply and demand). In economics, the aggregate demand of the potential buyers of a commodity or service.

market, acceptance

> The buyers of bank acceptances, including many banks, bankers, business firms, and corporations in the United States. Several corporations have been organized to deal primarily in acceptances and to bring buyers and sellers together.

market analysis

> A subdivision of marketing research, concerned with measuring the extent and characteristics of a given market's possibilities.

market penetration

> A term describing the degree to which an advertised product captures a percentage of the market for the product.

market position

> The image projected by a product which is intended to attract a particular consumer market.

market potential

> The possible sales of a commodity or service in a given market during a stated period.

market segmentation

> The division of a market into smaller categories, based on demographic and psychographic characteristics, in order to effectively market the product.

market share

> A company's percentage of sales of a product as compared to industry sales for the product.

market value

> The worth of a product or service as determined by what someone will pay for it at any particular time.

marketing

> The business activities which are concerned with the flow of goods and services from producer to consumer.

marketing campaign

> The coordination of all the efforts of the sales and advertising departments into one organized joint effort to market a company's product successfully.

marketing functions

> Tasks which are performed in the process of getting goods from the producer to the consumer. Some of the functions are selling, advertising, promoting, transporting, storing, financing, and assuming risks.

marketing mix

>The combination of decisions that have into the marketing of a good or service, including decisions on what product to sell at what price, what channels of distribution to use, and what promotional policies to employ.

marketing plan

>A program covering all the methods and procedures to be used in getting a product or a service from the producer to the consumer.

marketing policy

>A course of action established to secure consistency of marketing procedure under recurring and essentially similar circumstances.

marketing research

>The gathering, recording and analyzing of facts relating to the transfer and sale of goods and services from producer to consumer.

markup

>The difference between the selling price and the cost of a product.

Massachusetts Trust

>An investment company in which a number of investors turn over funds to a small group of trustees for management. The investors receive trust shares which are similar to corporate stock.

mass market

>The large potential buying public for a product which is widely used such as the market for soap as distinguished from the limited market for a product such as a machine tool.

mass marketing inquiries

>Inquiries generated by print ads, direct mail, or broadcast or television ads to the general public.

mass production

>The large-scale production of goods with standardized parts which can be interchangeable. The objective is lower unit costs, lower prices and more sales.

mass selling

>The selling of goods or services on a large scale such as to the general public.

master schedule

>An over-all production plan which indicates the number and various types of scheduled products which will be produced by the plant in stated future periods such as by week or by month.

materials

>The parts, goods, stock, or components of which anything is composed.

materials flow

>The path of movement of materials and parts from place to place during a manufacturing operation.

materials shortage

> A lack or deficiency of raw crude, or semi-processed materials necessary for making a certain product.

maternity benefits

> Insurance protection that specifically covers the costs of pregnancy, childbirth, post-partum care, family planning, and the like.

maternity leave

> The time off from work allotted to women for childbirth and a reasonable time afterwards.

matrice

> Also called a mat. A soft paper-like composition used as a mod to make stereotypes for newspaper printing.

matrix

> A graphic display of solutions to problems or situations under varying conditions.

mats

> The same as a matrice. See definition of matrice.

maturity date

> The date on which a note, time draft, bill of exchange, bond or other instrument becomes due and payable.

maximil rate

> The milline rate of a newspaper when it is calculated on the basis of the flat rate charged by the newspaper without time or volume discounts.

MBA

> Master of Business Administration degree.

MBWA

> See definition of management by walking around.

mechanical-aptitude tests

> Personnel tests which measure marketable skills, such as an applicant's proficiency in typing expressed in terms of speed and accuracy.

mechanization

> The degree to which work is performed by machines in a company, an industry, or a nation.

media

> The plural of medium. See definition of medium.

median

> That point above and below which there are an equal number of cases. A type of average which divides a group in half, the same number above as below.

mediation

> In collective bargaining this term refers to the action of an impartial third party who attempts to bring labor and management to a point of common agreement. The suggestions of a mediator are not binding on either party.

Medicaid

> A federally funded, state operated program in the U.S. which provides medical benefits to low income persons in need of care.

Medicare

> A national health insurance program in the U.S. which provides medical and hospital benefits to the elderly and disabled.

medium

> A channel or means of communication, such as radio, television, newspapers, billboards, or direct mail, used to reach the public for advertising, public relations, and the like.

medium of exchange

> Anything used as money in order to expedite the trading of goods and services between interested parties.

megabyte (Mbyte)

> Approximately one million bytes. Used when describing a system's storage capability.

memorandum

An inter-office or inter-company written communication, similar to a letter or informal report, which usually follows a predetermined form in the introductory section showing who originated it, to whom it is addressed, the subject matter and the date.

memory

The area within a computer where programs and data in current use are kept, usually on semiconductor circuits.

mentor

In management, an upper level manager who takes particular interest in the career advancement of a junior level manager and gives advice and direction to further that aim.

menu

A listing of available choices in a software program.

mercantile

Anything pertaining to merchants or trade.

merchandise

Goods, commodities, wares, or anything bought, sold, or exchanged.

merchandise manager

A type of supervisor in a department or specialty store who oversees the activities of buyers.

merchandising

> Retail policies which are designed to bring about reduced operating costs, such as sales for cash only, no-delivery service, and vigorous exploitation.

merchant

> A businessperson whose purpose is to buy and sell goods for a profit.

merchant middleman

> One who takes title to the goods stocked and sold, such as a wholesaler or a retailer. See middleman, merchant.

merger

> The taking over of one or more corporations by another in such a way that the absorbing company retains its identity and assumes the rights, privileges, franchises and properties of the other companies which cease to exist as separate entities.

merit increase

> A pay raise based on improved or exceptional performance, as distinguished from a cost of living increase which is defined elsewhere.

merit rating

> The assessing of employees in repect to their worth, value, ability to do the job, and the like.

methods improvement

> A management control technique used to improve production methods and eliminate waste.

MICR

> Abbreviation for magnetic ink character reader. A device used in banking to read the magnetic ink codes on bank checks. Can only read digits.

microcomputer

> Also called a personal computer. A small computer, usually characterized as having not more than 256K bytes of storage (although this distinction may vary as technology changes). Micros have a wide variety of functions making them useful in homes, schools and businesses. Examples are the IBM PC and the Apple computer.

microfilm

> A method of storage whereby information is photographed by microfilm equipment which reduces it in size by as much as 40 to 1.

micromotion

> A method of studying work motions too quick for the human eye to detect by making a motion picture study of the work with a clock of special design placed near the worker. The motion picture can then be run in slow motion to detect unnecessary movements.

microprocessor

> The collection of circuits, etched onto a single chip, which provides the data processing power of a microcomputer.

middleman

> An individual or business concern specializing in activities which transfer the title of goods from producer to consumer.

middleman, agent

One who negotiates or assists in the purchase or sale of goods but who does not take title, as exemplified by a broker, commission merchant, manufacturer's agent, selling agent, or resident buyer.

middleman, functional

One who participates in the movement of goods from buyer to seller, or seller to buyer, without taking title.

middleman, merchant

A middleman who takes possession of the goods he or she handles. He or she usually arranges for shipment of goods, stores them temporarily, sells them, and delivers them to the buyer.

mid-life crisis

That stage in a person's life or career when he or she has deep feelings of personal or professional inadequacy or failure. Not everyone goes through such a period, but enough do to make the phenomenon noteworthy.

mill

A building containing machinery for rubbing, grinding or crushing, such as a paper mill or a grain mill. Also, a tenth of a cent or thousandth of a dollar.

milline rate

The rate per line per million readers of a newspaper. The line rate of a particular newspaper times a million divided by the circulation.

minicomputer

> A small computer having more storage capacity than a microcomputer but not as much as a mainframe. Often used to supplement an existing system.

minimil rate

> The milline rate of a newspaper when it is calculated on the basis of the rate charged by the newspaper after time and volume discounts.

minimum wage

> That amount, under the Fair Labor Standards Act, that is the smallest hourly wage an employee can be paid for services rendered.

minutes of the meeting

> An official written record of what was said and what occurred at a meeting, convention, or assemblage.

miscellaneous

> A term used to classify items of several different categories which are too insignificant or too few to classify in separate categories.

missionary salesman

> A salesperson whose pricipal duty is to develop goodwill by assisting dealers to merchandise or sell to the consumer.

mobile unit

> A piece of equipment designed to be easily moved, such as a transformer on wheels.

mode

> An aspect of a computer program, or a system, dedicated to a particular activity. A program may have an "entry" mode, when data is entered; a "format" mode when data is organized; and a "print" mode when data is printed. Also, in statistics this term refers to an average which measures the number occurring most frequently in any given series.

model balance sheet

> The preparation of an estimated balance sheet in order that form and content can be examined from an ideal point of view. Particular stress is put on clarity of presentation and accuracy of classifications.

modeling

> Identifying and using fixed and variable components (or costs) to determine probable outcomes to changes in economic or financial assumptions.

modem

> A data communications device that changes analog signals to digital signals and vice-versa. Stands for modulator/demodulator.

modulation

> Converting a computer's digital signal into waveforms which can be carried by standard electronic media, such as telephone wire, microwave and coaxial cable.

module

> Part of a program designed for a specific task.

Mom and Pop shop

    Also, Mom and Pop store. An establishment owned and operated by a husband and wife and other members of their family. Usually describes small grocery stores, newspaper stands, and other neighborhood facilities.

money

    That which passes freely from hand to hand throughout the community in payment for goods and services and in full discharge of debts, being accepted without reference to the character or credit of the person offering it, and without the intention of the person who receives it to consume it otherwise than in tendering it to others.

money, cheap

    Money during a time when low interest rates prevail. Money whose value is low with respect to the amount of goods and services it will buy.

money, coined

    A piece of metal stamped and issued by the authority of the government for use as money.

money, earnest

    Money given by a buyer to a seller to bind a bargain.

money, fiat

    Money created by the government, the value of which is independent of the material from which it is made. Such money does not promise redemption in any other money.

money, functions of

A medium of exchange, a measure of value, a storehouse of value and a standard of deferred payments.

money, paper

Money made of paper and recognized by the government as legal tender for the payment of debt.

money changer

A person whose business is to exchange money from the currency of one nation to that of another. A person engaged in foreign exchange.

money market

A market for the trading of short-term investments such as U.S. Treasury bills and notes, commercial paper, certificates of deposit (CD's), Euro-dollar CD's and other debt instruments with less than a one-year duration.

money market mutual fund

A high-yield, short-term investment fund which represents a group investment in various money market instruments. Commercial banks and thrift organizations offer money market funds that are Federally insured and therefore not much riskier than a regular bank deposit.

money order

An instrument purchased in a bank or post office, used to send money out of town or by mail. The names of the purchaser and the payee appear on the instrument.

monitor

A video display screen.

monochromatic

Color in advertising in which only one basic color is used and harmony is attained by using various shades or tints of that color.

monopoly

An organization or combination of businesses within an industry controlling enough of the total business to be able to control supply, dictate prices, or curb competition.

monopoly power

The ability to exercise some or all of the elements of monopoly, such as controlling prices by restricting supply.

monopoly price

A price which is set on a good or service within an industry as the result of restricting the supply.

monotype

A typesetting machine which selects, sets, and spaces one slug at a time.

montage

A composition of camera shots or strips of images flashed in sequence so that the idea conveyed to the viewer is more than the sum of the material in the shots.

montage, photo

> A composit photograph, for decoration or publicity, made from the juxtaposition of cut-up photographs arranged in a pattern.

moonlighting

> Working at a second, usually part-time, job in addition to one's regular, full-time job.

morale, employee

> The collective feeling of employees about their company. There is a high degree of correlation between morale, efficiency, and productiveness.

mortality rate

> The percentage of people, calculated by age groups, who die during a specific period of time, computed as a basis for establishing life insurance rates.

mortality table

> A statistical analysis showing how many deaths out of a given sample, or what percentage of deaths, will occur at each year based on previous death rates and actuarial forecasting.

mortgage

> A document creating a lien on property, given to secure a promissory note.

mortgage, blanket

> The same as general mortgage. See definition of mortgage, general.

mortgage, chattel

> A mortgage on personal property, such as on automobiles or refrigerators. Also a mortgage on such goods as railroad equipment.

mortgage, closed-in

> A bond issue, secured by real estate, which is sold all at one time as distinguished from an open-end mortgage which is defined elsewhere.

mortgage, general

> Sometimes called a blanket mortgage. A corporate mortgage covering all the property of a business.

mortgage, open-end

> A bond issue, secured by real estate, which permits the sale of additional bonds.

mortgage, real estate

> A mortgage on real estate, including both lands and buildings.

motion study

> The breaking down of a job into all the motions a worker uses, such as reaching, selecting, picking up, and replacing in order to discover the rhythm of movement, distances covered, coordination, and sequence.

motivation research

> A form of market research which attempts to establish scientifically what makes consumers buy what they buy.

mouse

> An input device used with a computer to enter data without using a keyboard.

MS-DOS

> The most popular operating system for 16-bit microcomputers, based on the Intel 8086 and 8088 chips.

MTBF

> Abbreviation for mean time between failures. The length of time that a particular piece of equipment is expected to perform before requiring a repair.

multilith

> The same as photo-offset. See definition of photo-offset.

multiplexer

> A component which combines several signals from computers, or other electronic devices, into a single signal for economy of transmission.

multiplier

> The ratio of total change in national income to the change in new investment.

multiprocessing

> The ability of a computer system, consisting of more than one CPU linked together, to facilitate concurrent processing of various programs

or instructions. This differs from multiprogramming which is defined elsewhere.

multiprogramming

This term describes the capability of a computer system to process various programs and instructions simultaneously. This differs from multiprocessing in that multiprogramming refers to a computer system that includes a single CPU. See also multiprocessing.

mutual fund

The same as an investment trust. See definition of investment trust.

mutual insurance company

An insurance company which is owned by its policyholders as distinguished from a stock insurance company which is defined elsewhere.

N

nanosecond

> One billionth of a second. Used to describe the speed at which some computers operate.

national advertising

> The advertising of merchandise in all or several parts of the nation under a trade mark that identifies the manufacturer or distributor. From the point of view of local media, national advertising is advertising which identifies a manufacturer, a distributor, or a product rather than the individual local retailer who sells the product.

National Labor Relations Board (NLRB)

> A federally appointed agency which settles labor disputes between unions and employers.

near money

> Assets such as United States bonds and various kinds of savings accounts which can quickly be converted to cash.

necessities

> Goods and services considered as essential to a particular standard of living or to a person engaged in a particular kind of occupation.

negative stimulants

> Methods, generally considered undesirable, of stimulating employees to greater efforts. Negative stimulants are penalties or threats such as reprimand, transfer, reduced compensation or the threat of dismissal.

negligence

> Failure to use reasonable care to prevent or protect another party from injury.

negotiable instrument

> A written document expressing some contractual obligation which, by endorsement, can be transferred from one person to another.

negotiation

> The act of conferring with another or others for the purpose of coming to terms or of arriving at a basis of agreement.

nepotism

> The practice of awarding jobs or contracts to relatives, sometimes to the exclusion of other applicants who are equally well qualified.

net income

> The amount of money remaining after adding all revenues and gains and deducting all costs and expenses, including income tax expenses. If costs and expenses exceed revenues, a net loss has occurred.

net loss

> The deficit a business shows after the cost of goods sold and operating expenses, including administrative and selling expenses, have been

deducted from net sales. The final figure on an income income statement if a company has lost money for the accounting period.

net sales

Generally defined as gross sales minus returns and allowances. Some firms also deduct trade discounts and shipping costs.

net worth

The proprietor's equity in a business as represented by the excess of total assets over total liabilities. In a corporation, the total paid-in capital, earned surplus, and accumulated surplus.

network

Any group of computers or other electronic devices which can communicate with each other. Local area networks exist within single or nearby buildings, while remote networks may use satellites to communicate across continents. Also a verb: "to network" computer X with computer Y.

network radio

Radio programming which is carried simultaneously on a number of broadcast stations who are joined together into an association called a network.

networking

The process of making important contacts through various business associates. In some cities, networking luncheons and seminars are set up in which attendees are asked to pay a small fee to gain entrance and then have a chance to mingle with other networkers. Executives routinely exchange business cards at such meetings in order to expand their network of contacts.

newsletter

An informal report and analysis of the news, made up in a letter format and distributed at periodic intervals.

news release

A method of obtaining publicity by distributing to newspapers and other media a news story or an item of interest related to a business firm.

Nielsen survey

Also known as audimeter survey. See definition of audimeter.

NLRB

See definition of National Labor Relations Board.

node

A term referring to a terminal in a network.

non-compete clause

A clause inserted into a personal service contract so that the employee promises that if, per chance, he leaves his current employer, he will not go to work for a competitor in the same industry. The concept is based upon the idea that one doesn't want one's competitor to steal away a top executive in order to glean highly-sensitive company secrets. Most non-compete clauses have a duration of anywhere from one year to three years in effect.

nonforfeiture values

Certain privileges which the law requires be granted to the holder of an insurance policy in the event he decides to allow the policy to lapse. These are: (1) cash surrender value, (2) extended term insurance, or (3) paid-up insurance.

nonimpact printer

A computer output device that uses laser, heat or photographic technology to produce printed copy.

nonnotification plan

The act of pledging accounts receivable for a loan without notifying the accounts.

nonoperating company

A corporation not engaged in operating activities such as production and marketing. A holding company is usually a nonoperating company.

nonrecourse paper

A conditional sales contract which a dealer endorses to a finance company, specifying that the finance company cannot come back to the dealer to collect if the original debtor does not meet payments.

no-par stock

A stock certificate which does not have any definite worth printed on its face.

no protest (N.P.)

A statement written on a note indicating to a collecting bank that it should not protest in case of nonpayment. See definition of notice of protest.

note

> A written promise to pay a debt.

note, bank

> A written promise to pay to a bank holding a note, a certain sum of money on or before a certain date.

note, Federal Reserve

> A form of United States paper money. Currency issued by the Federal Reserve banks.

note, promissory

> A written promise to pay a specified amount at a specified time or place, or upon demand of a second party.

note, United States

> A form of Treasury currency. Paper money which is a remnant of Civil War financing.

notes and accounts receivable

> Amounts due the company from its customers.

notes payable

> Signed notes that represent or evidence a debt.

notice of dishonor

> An oral or written notification to makers, endorsers and drawers that a

negotiable instrument has not been paid when presented at the proper time.

notice of protest

A declaration made before a notary public that a check, bill of exchange or note has been presented and payment has been refused.

notification plan

The act of pledging accounts receivable for a loan and notifying the accounts of the action. When this is done, the various accounts are usually instructed to send their payments directly to the finance company making the loan.

N.P.

Abbreviation for no protest. See definition of no protest.

object program

> A program that has been translated into machine language for the computer to understand and run.

obsolescence

> The condition or process by which units gradually cease to be useful or profitable as part of property because of economic, social or technological changes.

obsolete

> An asset which has ceased to be useful or profitable due to social, economic or technological changes.

occupational disease

> An illness associated with performance of a job, such as black lung disease which affects coal miners.

occupational hazard

> A danger inherent in the performance of a job.

Occupational Safety and Health Administration (OSHA)

> A U.S. federal agency which makes and enforces rules regarding safety and health practices in the workplace.

OCR

> Abbreviation for optical character recognition. Using computerized systems to read printed characters, which can then be stored along with other data.

odd-lot

> The sale of stocks involving less than the established share-unit of trading. For most stocks this is less than 100 shares; for some it is less than 10 shares.

OEM

> Abbreviation for original equipment manufacturer.

off the books

> A slang term meaning to be paid for services rendered with no record of the payment being kept by the employer. The purpose is for both parties to avoid taxation.

offer

> The quotation of a seller for the sale of a trading unit or other specified amount of a security.

office

> The brain and nerve center of an organization where original records are prepared, reports are compiled, cost and statistical data are accumulated, records are maintained and retained, staff and service functions are performed, and business communications are handled.

office automation

> The integration of electronic equipment, such as computers and word processors, into the typical office environment, to improve information processing and administrative functions.

office manager

> A person who supervises and directs clerical employees in a business firm.

office personnel

> Employees of a busines firm who work in offices doing such tasks as collecting, processing, recording and transmitting information.

office routine

> Work which is performed regularly in a business office, requiring a minimum of mental exertion.

officer

> A person holding a position specified as official in a corporation's charter, by-laws or board resolutions.

offline

> Not actively connected to a computer system at a specific point in time.

old-age and survivors benefits

> A federal government insurance plan related to social security, providing an income for workers when they reach retirement age. The money for the plan comes from a joint contribution from employers and employees.

old-age assistance

> Benefits, administered by the various states, intended to provide help to needy or aged persons who are not inmates of public institutions. The federal government shares in the expense of these plans.

old boys' network

> A slang expression referring to a group of businessmen who, due to previous association in schools or clubs, continue to help each other in business by giving contracts, or hiring friends of those in the "network," as opposed to other qualified persons.

oligopoly

> A condition in an economy in which total production in an industry is confined to a few producers.

one-price house

> A retail establishment which adheres to a uniform selling-price policy, selling at the same price to all customers.

online

> Actively functioning as a part of a computer system at a specific point in time. A terminal or printer may be offline for some hours or days, then be online for another period of time.

open-book account

> A short-term charge account either of a business or of an ultimate consumer for which there is no interest charged and no distinction between cash price and credit price.

open door policy

> A traditional policy in which the manager announces to his staff that "my door is always open" in case any particular employee has a suggestion or comment and wants to let the manager know how he or she feels.

open-end investment company

> Also called an investment trust. A company which commits itself to repurchase the shares of a holder at any time upon demand. It offers shares for sale continuously and issues a single class of stock. The price of shares is based on the total market value of the securities in the portfolio divided by the number of shares outstanding.

open-end investment trust

> See definition of investment trust.

open-end question

> In marketing, a survey question that allows respondents to answer in their own words, as distinguished from a closed-end question which is defined elsewhere.

open house

> A special public-relations event undertaken by a business firm in which the business opens its doors to the public for inspection of its offices or plant.

open shop

> A company which employs both union an non-union workers.

operant conditioning

>A term used in management to describe an approach to motivating employees which focuses on stimulus, response and reward.

operating expenses

>The costs of running a business that are incurred in ordinary business activities such as administrative expenses, production costs, sales and marketing expenses and the like.

operating income

>The income realized from normal operations, before computing any extraordinary gains or losses.

operating loss

>The loss realized from normal business operations, before the addition of any extraordinary gains or losses.

operating system

>That part of a computer's control unit that directs certain tasks to be done automatically without user intervention.

operation

>A mathematical or logical process performed by a computer.

operation sheets

>A standard list, for each part or assembly, of all operations necessary to convert a piece of raw material, or a collection of parts, into a finished part or assembly.

operations research

> A method of using mathematical and statistical data, supplied by an electronic computer, to make managerial decisions in such fields as budgeting and forecasting.

opinion survey

> The orderly process of determining, through interviews, the personal evaluation, attitudes or preferences of a selected group of respondents. A type of marketing research.

optical scanner

> An input device that reads characters, codes or symbols and converts them into a form that can be processed by a computer.

option

> An agreement to hold an offer open for a specified period of time in return for a consideration.

optional modes of settlement

> Provision in a life insurance policy for payment of the face value of an insurance policy in various ways other than a lump sum.

order, limit

> In investments this expression refers to an authorization to a broker to buy or sell only at a certain price or better.

organization

> The process of arranging a business into units and of assigning authority and responsibility to each unit. A business firm.

organization chart

A diagram or graphic representation depicting the structure of a business firm, including the titles and units at each level.

organized labor

A term referring to all labor unions, collectively.

OSHA

See definition of Occupational Safety and Health Administration.

outlet

A market for a commodity. A retail or wholesale establishment from which goods are sold.

outplacement

The policy of helping an employee who has been dismissed to find a new job. Usually this consists of directing the employee to an employment agency, vocational training center, career counseling, and the like.

output

The quantity or amount produced by a factor of production. Or, information produced by a computer.

output unit

Any device, such as a printer or CRT, that receives information from a computer and converts it into hard or soft copy output.

overcapitalized

The state of a corporation which has too much capital invested in relation to expected earnings.

overdraw

To draw checks in excess of the amount deposited in a bank.

overhead

Non-specific expenses, such as light, heat and rent, which cannot be directly related to any particular unit of production.

overhead, factory

Those factory costs which are impossible or impractical to identify with a specific unit of production.

overproduction

The output of a business firm which is above that which will readily be absorbed by the market or above the amount which can be distributed at a normal rate.

over-the-counter

The purchase or sale of unlisted securities which do not trade on a stock exchange.

over-the-counter market

The market for securities not traded on exchanges but sold and purchased by dealers who effect the transactions over the telephone.

overtime

    Daily hours of work in excess of the number established by contract or by law for which wage earners normally receive extra pay.

owners' equity

    Also, stockholders' equity. The owners' or stockholders' interest in a company, represented by the company's total assets minus total liabilities.

P

package deal

    The same as a combination sale. See definition of combination sale.

package engineering

    An applied science concerned with the art of designing containers for products.

packaging

    The process of wrapping, enveloping, and cushioning material to protect it from damage. The wrapping of material in an attractive container in order to stimulate sales.

page printer

    A computer output device that prints out one page at a time.

paid-up insurance

    An alternative to the cash-surrender value of a life-insurance policy, providing a flat amount of permanent insurance based on the attained age of the insured and the amount of cash-surrender value at the time the policy lapses.

panel discussion

    A conference held by persons who are brought together to consider a particular subject.

paper, bond

    A firm, uncalendered paper made of superior stock, originally used for printing security bonds but now used for stationery and the like.

paper, carbon

    A relatively strong paper with carbon ink deposited on it, used in making duplicate impressions on underlying sheets of typed material.

paper, cash

    Currency or paper money issued by a government through an act of law. Legal tender.

paper, ledger

    A paper somewhat the same as bond but heavier, more easily erased and with a harder surface. It is used for ledgers, journals, and other posted records.

paper, manifold

    The same as onion skin paper. See definition of paper, onion skin.

paper, mimeo bond

    A grade of paper used for duplication from a stencil.

paper, onion skin

Also called manifold paper. A lightweight bond paper, useful in making numerous carbon copies.

paper, safety

A paper with a surface treatment which reveals attempted alterations, used for such things as checks, certificates and negotiable instruments.

paper loss

The decline in market value of a security since it was purchased. This loss is unrealized until the security is sold and the loss becomes real.

paper profit

The appreciation in market value of a security since it was purchased. The profit is unrealized.

parallel interface

A line between computers and/or printers, modems and other devices which carries more than one bit at a time. On an 8-bit system, a parallel interface carries 8 bits at a time; on a 16-bit system, 16 bits; etc.

parcel post insurance

A form of inland marine insurance covering "all-risk" and extending from the time the property comes into the custody of the post office until the merchandise is surrendered by the post office at its stated destination.

parent company

A company which controls one or more subsidiaries.

parity

A price established, especially for farm goods, designed to give the seller the equivalent in buying power to that which existed during a past period of time, called the base period.

parity bit

A bit used by the computer to check for errors in data transmission. See also parity check.

parity check

A method of determining errors in data. In even parity, the computer adds up a given number of bits (represented by either a 0 or a 1) and, if the sum is even, it adds a 0 so the sum remains even. The data is then transmitted and checked again at its destination. If the quantity of data comes up odd, error is assumed and, depending on the system, action will be taken. Parity checks can be even or odd.

partial registration

An expression used to refer to a type of coupon bond wherein the owner is registered to protect him against loss of the principal due to theft. Anyone, however, can collect interest without showing evidence of ownership by presenting the coupon.

partner, junior

A partner in a business who does not have a relatively large amount of money invested in the enterprise, receives a minor share of the profits, and does not assume responsibility for major decisions.

partner, senior

A partner in a business who has a relatively large amount of money invested in the enterprise, receives a large share of the profits, and makes major decisions.

partner, silent

Also called a dormant partner and a sleeping partner. A member of a partnership who does not play an active role in the business and who is not known to the public as a partner.

partnership

An association of two or more persons acting together in a business undertaking and combining their capital, labor, and materials for the purpose of profit.

partnership, limited

A type of partnership in which one or more members do not assume unlimited liability.

partnership, mining

A special business organization permitted by some states for persons engaged in mining operations or in drilling oil, allowing a partner to transfer or sell his shares without dissolving the business. A form of stock is usually issued, and profits are distributed in proportion to shares held.

part shift

An arrangement whereby workers are allowed to work only part of a shift.

PASCAL

A popular programming language for microcomputers and minicomputers (named for Blaise Pascal). Uses structured programming techniques.

pass the dividend

The act of a board of directors deciding not to pay a dividend to preferred stockholders for a particular fiscal period.

past due account

A receivable that remains uncollected after the payment terms expire.

patent

An exclusive privilege for 17 years to control the sale and use of an invention.

patent pool

An agreement among several companies to share the use of patents, frequently employed as a means of combining in restraint of trade.

patent release

A form signed by an employee, certifying that he or she will turn over to the company any patentable ideas he or she develops.

pay, deferred

Pay which is earned but withheld from payment until a future date.

pay, separation

>The final settlement of money due and earned, paid at the time a worker's employment is terminated.

payee

>The person or firm in whose favor a note is drawn.

payroll

>A list of persons paid or entitled to be paid, showing the net amount due each and the total amount necessary for distribution to those listed.

payroll deductions

>Deductions from an employee's wages made by an employer for such items as income taxes, old age and survivors benefits, group-insurance premiums and union dues.

payroll sheets

>A form recording the accumulation of hours and earnings of employees within a department, used to balance the weekly payroll.

PBX

>Abbreviation for private branch exchange. A telephone switching system for use within the office, owned (or leased) by the company which uses it rather than by a telephone company. Can be used to transfer data between computers as well as to carry voice conversation.

PC-DOS

>A disk operating system to be used with the IBM Personal Computer.

pecking order

    A slang term referring to the informal ranking of people in organizations.

pecuniary interest

    Having a monetary interest in something.

peddler car

    A service provided by a railroad whereby a freight car drops off goods of a single shipper to a number of customers in different locations along the route.

pension

    A payment made regularly to a person who has fulfilled certain conditions of service, reached a certain age, or is disabled.

pension fund

    A trust fund established to pay retirement benefits to employees of a business firm. Periodic payments are made under contract to the fund according to a trust agreement.

per capita income

    A statistical proportionment of aggregate income to each individual. In calculating per capita income, total income of a group is divided by the number of persons in the group.

percent

    A quantity or amount measured by the number of units in proportion to one hundred.

per diem

An amount of money paid per day for expenses incurred by an employee engaged in affairs of the business away from his or her regular place of work.

performance appraisal

A periodic objective evaluation of an employee's work effort conducted by the employee's supervisor using objective measures or criteria. A performance appraisal usually accompanies one's salary increment.

peripheral

A secondary component, such as a color monitor, modem or printer, which is attached to a computer.

perquisites (perks)

Benefits received by employees beyond those of compensation and insurance coverage. Perks might include a company car, tickets to sporting events, free lunches and the like.

personal computer

Same as microcomputer. See microcomputer.

personal property

Also called personalty. The things owned which are movable as distinguished from real property which is immovable.

personal property, intangible

Movable property in the form of stocks, bonds, notes and checks as distinguished from tangible personal property which is defined elsewhere.

personal property, tangible

Movable property in the form of machinery, equipment, and the like, as distinguished from intangible personal property which is defined elsewhere.

personal property floater

A form of inland marine insurance, which is an "all risk" policy, covering personal belongings of the insured and his family.

personalty

The same as personal property. See definition of personal property.

personnel

The employees of a business organization.

personnel management

The management of employees as individuals as distinguished from industrial relations which deals with employees as groups. It has to do with planning, directing, and coordinating such activities as securing, training, and utilizing employees.

PERT

Acronym for program evaluation and review technique. A management tool designed to facilitate planning and scheduling by using a graphic network diagram of the "time-path" relationships among activities making up a project. PERT is concerned primarily with the probability of completing a project within a specified time. Also called CPM (critical path method).

petition

Any undertaking or request made to a court of justice for the purpose of receiving some sort of relief. A written application as distinguished from a motion.

photo-offset

Also known as planograph or multilith. A process of duplication using photography to prepare a negative from which a plate of soft metal or of paper is made. The plate is so treated that some portions will accept ink, others reject it. The inked image is transferred to a rubber blanket and then impressed on paper.

physical plant

The fixed assets of a business firm, such as land, buildings, and equipment, used in the production process.

pica

A standard of measure for type. A pica is one-sixth of an inch long or 12 point. One square inch contains 36 square picas. One square pica and the 12 point em are identical.

picketing

The act by workers of having one or more persons at the entrances to a plant to inform the public that a strike is in progress.

picosecond

One trillionth of a second. Used to describe the speed at which some computers can operate.

picture continuity

A public relations tool known more familiarly as a comic book. See definition of picture panel.

picture panel

A comic book or picture continuity used as a method of communicating with employees, customers, unions or the general public.

piece rate

An incentive wage rate which is designed to pay a worker in proportion to his or her unit output.

piece wage

Pay given to a worker on the basis of so much per each unit of output.

piggyback

A railroad service which provides trucks which will ride on railroad flat cars. This, in effect, reduces the number of times goods must be loaded and unloaded. In advertising the term refers to the practice of placing radio or television advertisements back to back.

pilfering

The act of committing petty thievery. Petty theft of business property committed by employees.

pipe lines

A system of transportation via pipes, used to move products such as petroleum from the producing areas to the major distributing and refining areas.

pits

The central locations in a grain exchange where buying and selling are conducted by members of the exchange.

placement

The placing of a person in a job, assigning work usually on a probationary basis.

placement bureau

A business organization or a department within a business firm whose function is to place employees in occupations best suited to their temperament and ability.

plaintiff

In civil law this term refers to a person who files a complaint (in Canada, a writ) or a statement of claim in court, setting out the facts which led to the controversy for which judgment is asked.

planning section

The department in the production process which schedules work so that it will be completed on time and economically.

planograph

The same as photo-offset. See definition of Photo-offset.

pledge

In commercial law this term refers to a form of lien. A debtor turns over to a creditor an article of personal property to hold as collateral until a loan is paid.

pledged securities

> The pledging of stocks and bonds as collateral for a debt.

PLI

> A high level programming language for large computers that combines features of both Fortran and COBOL.

plotter

> A printing device used for creating drawings and graphics, with one or more pens which may be of different colors.

plural-voting stock

> Stock which has more than one vote per share. This is often founders' shares, issued to promoters to enable them to retain control of the business they organized.

point system

> A method of job evaluation in which a number of factors is established in order to analyze a job. Each factor is assigned points and thus is weighed in relation to the others.

policy, company

> The guide or plans for conducting the affairs of a business, established by the board of directors and carried out by the operating officers through the workforce.

pool

> A method of eliminating competition wherein several companies sign a written agreement covering one or more phases of mutual operation,

such as the prices they will charge, the disposition of territories or the amount which each company will produce.

pool, output

An agreement among two or more companies, covering the percentage of total output which each will manufacture.

pool, price and profit

An agreement among two or more companies to charge certain prices and to share profits on a percentage basis.

pool, territorial

An agreement among two or more companies, covering the geographical market or markets which each will develop on an exclusive basis.

pool car service

A service provided by railroads which allows a shipper, who is shipping a carload of goods to a number of consignees along the route, to take advantage of carload rates to the first receiver and less than carload lot rates to the rest.

port

A physical location on a computer, terminal, printer, etc. where it can be connected to cables or other devices.

portfolio

The composite security holdings of a person or corporation. The reinsurance held by an insurance carrier.

position

    The job held by a person. The duties and responsibilities assigned to a person hired by a business organization.

posting

    The process in accounting of transferring the information recorded in the book of original entry to the accounts which are kept in a separate book called the ledger.

posting reference

    In accounting this expresion refers to cross references of pages between the journal and the ledger for each transaction.

power of attorney

    The granting by a formal written document of the right to an agent to act in behalf of a principal.

precision manufactured

    A product which has been made to minutely exact specifications.

preemptive right

    The right of a stockholder to purchase a proportion of any addition issue of stock in order to maintain his or her relative ownership in the corporation.

preferential union shop

    A company in which the employer has agreed to give preference to union members in hiring and laying off workers.

preferred stock

A type of ownership stock which pays a stated rate of annual return as a dividend as distinguished from common stock which is defined elsewhere.

premium

The amount paid for insurance protection against a risk. In bonds, a premium is the difference between the face value and a higher market price.

premium, annual

The cost of an insurance policy paid for in advance on a yearly basis.

premium, monthly

The cost of an insurance policy broken down on a monthly basis as a convenience to buyers. For most plans, this cost is based on an annual rate plus interest and handling charges divided by 12.

premium pay

Extra wages or bonuses paid to workers for overtime, working nights, and the like.

presentment

See definition of due presentment.

present worth

The discount or current value of a sum of money due and payable at a specified future date. For example, at 6% interest, the present worth of $106 in one year is $100.

president

> The head administrator of a business who directs the organization in carrying out policies established by the board of directors, and who represents the company in dealing with other organizations and with the government.

press agent

> A person whose job is to handle publicity and news releases for a business.

press conference

> An interview with members of the news media to provide them with information which might not otherwise be presented accurately and fully.

press kit

> A kit generally prepared by a public relations department, containing a variety of feature stories, glossy photographs, and articles related to news and information about a company.

price

> The value of a product or service expressed in terms of money.

price, actual

> The established or real price of something as distinguished from the nominal price.

price, equilibrium

> A price at which the quantity demanded equals the quantity supplied. A condition in which opposing economic forces are balanced.

price, nominal

> A stated price which is not the real price for which merchandise is offered.

price, normal

> The price which covers cost plus necessary (as compared with excessive) profit.

price ceiling

> The maximum price that can be asked for something. A price usually established by government regulation in extraordinary times, such as during a war where a severe inflation threatens the economy.

price controls

> The fixing of prices by the government or by private organizations. Also, efforts to restrict the freedom of markets by pegging the prices of things sold.

price cutting

> Lowering the price below the price recognized as normal in order to meet competition or to attract customers.

price fixing

> The freezing of prices at a stated level by the government or by private organizations in order to control inflation or deflation or to restrict the freedom of the market.

price lines

In retailing this expression is used to refer to a series of predetermined prices representing the only prices at which specific lines of merchandise will be offered for sale. All other intermediate prices for the merchandise are discarded.

price making

Establishing the pecuniary value of a product or service offered for sale.

price sensitivity

The degree to which the price charged for a product or service will effect the demand for that product or service.

price system

An economy in which the value of goods is expressed in terms of money.

price war

A severe lowering of price by one seller which other sellers must follow or beat in order to compete.

pricing

Setting the value of a commodity or service offered for sale.

primary data

Information which has been directly gathered by market research either from internal records or external research as distinguished from secondary data which is supplementary information based on indirect sources.

primary storage

>The main memory of a computer as distinguished from auxiliary or secondary storage which is defined elsewhere.

prime rate

>An advantageous interest rate for loans charged by banks to enterprises with strong credit standing.

principal

>The face amount of a note on which interest is calculated. Also a person who authorizes an agent to act in behalf of himself in dealing with third parties.

privileged subscriptions

>Offerings of stock or other securities to a corporation's own shareholders.

probationary period

>A period within which a person, newly assigned to a task or newly hired by a business firm, is allowed to prove himself or herself as satisfactory.

proceeds

>The amount remaining after a discount for interest has been deducted from the face value of a promissory note.

process

>The series of operations making up a completed plan of production.

process engineer

> A person who prepares instructions used by a planner in determining production operations. One who studies engineering blueprints and determines the various tool requirements for a job.

processing unit

> A part of a digital computer which performs the functions of control, decision-making, logic and arithmetic.

producer

> A person or company engaged in manufacturing or creating goods for a profit.

product

> A good manufactured by a producer for the purpose of receiving a profit.

product analysis

> A study of products through market research in order to develop new ones, adapt old ones to new uses, or to determine product characteristics most valuable to the consumer. Also, in industrial research, the studying of how to produce the best possible product for the most economical price.

product development

> The activities of a department in a business firm which receives reports of products, evaluates products from the standpoint of their marketability and makes recommendations to company heads.

product identification

A positive identification making a product stand out from others. Some means of product identification are trade marks, brand names, special names, packaging, stickers and labels.

product liability

The responsibility of a manufacturer to take reasonable care to protect the public from harm due to production of defective goods.

product life cycle

The stages of a product, as defined by its sales, from introduction, through growth and maturity, to decline and finally, discontinuation.

product line

The various products in which a manufacturer or seller specializes.

production

The manufacture of goods, including raw materials, semi-manufactured goods and finished products.

production, continuous-process

Production which is scheduled on a regular basis because the products are standard ones made for stock before orders are received.

production, factors of

Those things which are pertinent to the production process, such as labor, capital, machinery and land.

production, specific-order

> Production in which the manufacturing is based on specifications established by the buyer.

production, speculative

> The manufacture of goods before orders for them are received.

production committee

> A committee of shop foremen and representatives of the production-planning deparment, organized to discuss matters pertaining to the operation of the factory, the status of production orders, reasons for delay, and other pertinent production matters.

production control

> The proper use of people, materials and machinery in a business for the purpose of economically delivering goods to a customer at the time required, for a price the customer is willing and able to pay, and of a quality that will serve the customer's purpose.

production manager

> The person responsible for the manufacture of a firm's product.

production records

> The information preserved in writing pertaining to a business firm's productive output.

productive capacity

> The amount or volume of output which a business firm is capable of manufacturing.

products, joint

> Two or more products which result from the same manufacturing operation or series of operations.

profession

> A gainful occupation not classified as a business in which profit-making is not necessarily the primary goal. The three best known are law, medicine and theology. In recent years, other callings, such as engineering and architecture, have established claims to rank as professions.

profit

> The noncontractual share of income left to the enterpriser or the investor.

profit, net

> The noncontractual share of income realized by a business after cost of goods sold and expenses are deducted from revenue.

profit, operating

> The noncontractual share of income realized by a business from its regular activities as distinguished from profit realized from such things as outside investments.

profit, undivided

> The noncontractual share of business income which has not been distributed among stockholders or partners.

profit and loss statement

>Also known as an income statement. A detailed statement showing revenue less the cost of goods sold and other expenses with the resulting net profit to a firm for a specified period of time.

profit center

>A company unit whose operations can be measured in terms of profit.

profit margin

>A measure of the operating efficiency and profitability of a company, obtained by dividing its net income by its net sales.

profit motive

>The hope for gain which induces people to invest in a business enterprise.

profit sharing

>The dividing and distributing of a share of the profits either immediately or on a deferred basis, among company employees.

profit taking

>The act of selling investment securities in order to convert paper profits into cash.

program

>In computer language this term refers to a sequence of steps established for a computer in order to solve a problem.

projection

In statistics this term refers to the extension of a mathematical series beyond the range of observed data.

promoter

One who undertakes to launch a new business project, especially one who assumes responsibility for selling a new project's stock or securities in order to obtain necessary capital.

promotion

The advancement of an employee to a job requiring greater skill, more responsibility and more pay.

promotional allowance

The amount of money allocated by a company for the advertising, sales and promotion of its product or products.

prompt

A signal, usually indicated by a cursor, telling the user that the computer is ready to receive input.

proof

A trial printing used as the basis for changes and corrections before a final printing.

proofread

The act of reading a copy of printed matter before the final printing in order to detect and correct errors in typing, grammar and punctuation.

property, common

    Wealth owned by a community or by the general public.

property, community

    Real property in which a husband and wife together own an undivided interest - that is, an interest which cannot be shared without the consent of both parties.

property, private

    Wealth owned or in the exclusive possession of an individual.

property tax

    A tax imposed on real estate or on personal property by a state or local government.

proposition

    Anything put forward as a scheme or plan of action. Thus a sales proposition is one designed to persuade the prospect to take action.

proprietorship

    An unincorporated business with a sole owner.

pro rata

    A proportional distribution of an expense, dividend, or some other item on an equitable basis.

prospect

    A potential buyer, applicant, or customer.

prospectus

> A complete and detailed written description of a new security issue supplied to prospective purchasers.

prosperity

> A term used to designate that period of a business cycle during which the volume of production is large, consumer demand and ability to pay are high, and employment is at a peak level.

protest

> The same as notice of protest. See definition of notice of protest.

protocol

> The procedure used to access a computer system. Protocols vary depending on each given computer system.

provincial tax

> A tax levied by a Canadian province in order to raise revenue. Most frequently, such levies are on gasoline, personal income, corporations, and production.

proxy

> A written authorization to vote granted to another by a shareholder who will be absent from a stockholders' meeting.

proxy fight

> A struggle for control of a corporation through appeal to stockholders to send in their proxies to one or the other of the contending parties.

prudent man rule

    A state law allowing a trustee of an estate to purchase securities that a careful investor would buy for his own account.

psychographic characteristics

    In marketing, the personal traits that typify a market segment, such as behavior and lifestyle, personality, spending habits, and the like.

psychological need

    The need for a product or service which arises from the mental attitude of a consumer as distinguished from the actual physical necessity.

public

    People in general, such as the buying public.

public finance

    The financial operations of all levels of government, including budgeting, taxing, appropriating, purchasing, borrowing, disbursing funds, and regulating currency.

public market

    Sometimes called a farmers' market. An area such as a section of a city where farmers can bring their produce and sell it to ultimate consumers.

public opinion

    The attitude or feeling of the public in general about any particular good.

public relations

> The management function which evaluates public attitudes, identifies the policies and procedures of an individual organization with the public interest, and executes a program of action to earn public understanding and acceptance.

public relations stunt

> Or, P.R. stunt. Any kind of exhibition or display by a company in order to either capture the public's attention or to ingratiate the public to the company's product or service.

public utility

> A private enterprise engaged in producing, with a minimum of competition, a good or service regarded as important to the public welfare, such as electricity. Because of the widespread need for the product or service of a public utility, prices and many of its activities are regulated by the local or federal governments.

publicity

> Information, channeled through the various organs of communication, designed to advance the interests of a business firm, and differing from advertising in that it is generally released at little or no cost.

pulse survey

> A method of checking the effectiveness of advertising by interviewing a random sample of persons who may have been exposed to the message. The interview uses printed matter in order to aid the memory or recall of the interviewees.

pump-priming

> A method of stimulating business activity by government spending.

punch card machine

> A machine which transfers information from an original document to a card by punching holes in predetermined positions.

purchase order

> A formal signed buying statement sent to a vendor specifying what is being bought, the description of the goods, the unit prices, the quantities, the delivery dates, shipping instructions and other pertinent details.

purchase record

> A control form used by the purchasing department providing information about commodities which have been purchased.

purchase requisition

> A formal written request sent to a purchasing department, specifying supplies or materials to be ordered.

purchases, charge-take

> Procurements made on the basis of credit which are transported to the place of consumption by the buyer.

purchasing

> The act of procuring raw materials, semi-finished goods, finished products and services. The term refers to both wholesale and retail buying.

purchasing, centralized

> The act of procuring from a home office or from a single location for many different locations or branches of a business firm.

purchasing, contract

> The policy of buying by entering into agreements with suppliers for the delivery of materials over long periods of time.

purchasing, scheduled

> The placing of orders for materials in amounts up to a year's estimated usage with the arrangement that specified quantities of the total order be delivered each week or month.

purchasing, speculative

> The placing of orders for quantities of materials in excess of current needs, anticipating that prices are going to rise and that savings can be gained by buying ahead.

purchasing department

> The department of a business firm responsible for the procurement of goods and services.

purchasing power

> The same as buying power. See definition of buying power.

puts and calls

> In investment, these terms are used to signify options to buy or sell a stipulated number of securities at a specified price. A put is an option giving the holder the right to call on the maker to buy. A call is an option giving the holder the right to call on the maker to sell. See definition of maker.

pyramiding

> The process by which a holding company obtains, with relatively little investment, control over operating corporations, the effect of which is to have a series of companies branching downward, each owning controlling interest in the one under it.

Q

qualifications

>The requisites a person must possess in order to attain a position or status.

qualify

>In sales this term refers to the act of determining whether a possible prospect for a product or service is a real one. The word is also used in the sense of being worthy or trained for a job as "to qualify for a position."

quality circles

>Small groups of employees who meet regularly to discuss work problems and how to solve them.

quality control

>A system, including inspection, used in product design and production to insure uniform quality of product.

quartile

>The three values at the division points if items of an array are divided into four equal parts. Quintile is the term used if items are divided

into five equal parts, and decile is the term used if items are divided into ten equal parts.

query language

An easy-to-use language, similar to the English language, used to seek information from a database.

questionnaire

A set of questions used in testing individuals or groups of persons in order to get data desired or needed to make business decisions.

quick assets

Cash and call loans, marketable securities and other assets which can readily be converted into cash.

quintile

See definition of quartile.

quit

The act of resigning or separating oneself from employment.

quit claim deed

A form of title to property which transfers an interest a grantor has at the time but which contains no definite guarantee to title and which transfers no after-acquired interest.

quorum

A certain number of members of a group, board or committee, constituting a legally qualified number to transact business affairs.

quota system

In hiring, a term referring to a specific number of minority employees, such as blacks or women, that a company must employ in order to meet percentage regulations imposed by the EEOC in the enforcement of U.S. discrimination laws.

quotation record

A file of rates and other information related to vendors, maintained by the purchasing agent of a business firm.

R

rack-jobber

> A wholesaler specializing in items displayed on racks in supermarkets, retailing, etc.

raiding

> The procedure of buying up enough stock of a company and of conducting a proxy fight in order to capture control and take over its management.

RAM

> Acronym for random access memory. Computer memory used for storing data. Data stored in RAM can be altered or erased as distinguished from ROM, which is defined elsewhere.

random sampling

> An expression used in research, referring to a situation where each item or individual in the sample to be surveyed has an equal chance of being included.

range

> The difference between the highest and the lowest, such as the range in price for a security over a stated period of time.

rat race

> A slang term referring to the fast-paced business world and those who occupy it in an endless pursuit of monetary and material success.

rate card

> A card or folder issued by an advertising medium giving the space or time rates and other pertinent data related to the cost and the scope of the services rendered by the medium.

rate of exchange

> The price at which a bill of exchange is bought or sold in the so-called foreign exchange market located in the large financial centers of the world.

rate of return

> The interest yield which a corporation earns on total stockholder capital during a fiscal year.

rates, class

> A schedule of costs for shipping by rail various goods which are distinguished by descriptive categories.

rates, commodity

> A schedule of costs for shipping by rail various goods specified by name.

rates, exception

> A schedule of costs for shipping by rail goods which are classified as exceptions to class rates. Class rates are defined elsewhere.

rating, analytic

>A form of merit rating of personnel in which the person making the rating is asked to gauge an employee's performance according to a large number of small judgments.

rating scale

>A system of judging, during an interview, the qualifications or qualities of an applicant by grading him or her on a scale.

ratio

>The measure of a relation between two like quantities. The quotient arrived at by dividing one magnitude by another of the same kind.

ratio, acid test

>A ratio which relates the current liabilities of a business to cash plus receivables plus marketable securities in order to determine the ability of a business enterprise to meet its current obligations.

ratio, balance sheet

>Ratios based on analysis of a balance sheet or a series of balance sheets to determine the condition and growth of a business. Some of the common ratios are current assets to current liabilities, fixed liabilities to net worth, and net worth to capital stock.

ratio, current

>A ratio which relates current assets to current liabilities in order to determine the amount of working capital. This is sometimes called "the bankers' ratio" because bankers commonly use it in credit analysis.

ratio, debt

> One of several financial measurements of business condition. Calculated by dividing total debt by total assets.

ratio, financial

> The comparison of financial relationships as a means of determining the condition of a business and the problems it faces. Ratios which measure the relationship between two accounts or between groups of accounts.

ratio, inventory turnover

> The cost of goods sold for a year divided by the average value of the inventory.

ratio, liquidity

> A ratio which relates the holdings of cash to current liabilities in order to determine the degree to which a company can meet its immediate debts.

ratio, net worth

> Ratios which measure the relationship between investment and net worth of an enterprise.

ratio, operating

> A ratio which shows the relationship between the operating costs and operating revenue. Some companies include under the category of operating costs the selling expenses, the administrative expenses and the general expenses of the enterprise but not the cost of goods sold. Other companies include all of the expenses and costs, including the cost of goods sold.

ratio, price earnings

The ratio of market price of a company's stock to its earnings.

ratio, quick

Also called acid test ratio. See definition of ratio, acid test.

ratio, sales

Ratios which relate sales to various other factors of a business, such as inventory or fixed assets.

ratio, volume-expense-calls

A ratio which is used to evaluate a salesperson's performance on the basis of his or her cost per call and on the basis of the volume of sales he or she makes. The salesperson's net sales is multiplied by his or her expenses as a percent of sales. This figure is then divided by the number of calls. The quotient is the cost per call.

raw materials

Goods used in the industrial process which have undergone no more processing than is required for convenience or for economy in storing, transporting, or handling.

read

To retrieve data from a computer disk or tape.

real estate

Land and the rights associated with the land. Anything attached to the land by nature or by people.

real income

Income as measured by the quantity of goods and services which money will buy rather than by the amount of money received.

real property

Also called realty. Property which is immovable, such as land and buildings.

real time

The actual present tense of the computer user. The ability to operate in real time and respond immediately to users was an important factor in the growth of small computers, factory automation and telecommunications.

realty

The same as real property. See definition of real property.

rebate

The return of a portion of interest previously collected if a loan is paid off prior to maturity date. In insurance, this term refers to the illegal return of part of a premium payment by an agent to an insured.

recapitalization

The rearrangement of the capital structure of a corporation. For tax purposes, the term refers to a readjustment of the amount or priority of stocks and bonds, or an agreement of stockholders and debtors to decrease or increase the capital or debts of a corporation.

receiver

    A trustee of the property of a bankrupt company. A person who manages a bankrupt company for the benefit of creditors and stockholders, subject to the control and authority given him or her by the court.

receivership

    The condition of being in the hands of a receiver. An unpaid creditor may apply to equity for the appointment of a receiver to take over property of the debtor for the purpose of applying the property to the payment of the debts.

receiving department

    The department responsible for receiving materials and supplies and reporting their arrival to the purchasing department.

recession

    A period in the business cycle in which the economy is characterized by a tapering off of business activity from a period of prosperity.

reconcile

    The same as reconciliation of bank balance. See definition of reconciliation of bank balance.

reconciliation of bank balance

    The auditing of his or her monthly bank statement by a depositor. The depositor checks his or her records against the bank statement in order to correct any errors shown on the bank statement.

record

A group of related fields. See also character, field, file.

record, finished stock

A record of products ready for the final consumer, used to guide the plant manager in filling orders and in preventing the accumulation of obsolete stock.

recourse paper

An endorsement, on a discounted negotiable instrument, which makes the endorser liable as well as the original borrower. In effect the endorser agrees to pay in the event the borrower defaults.

recover

A stage of the business cycle where economic activity begins to pick up after a depression or recession. Labor conditions improve, wages go higher and jobs become easier to find.

recruitment

The process of seeking and obtaining people for employment.

redemption provision

An option allowing a corporation for a stated price to buy back a preferred stock or to redeem a bond before its maturity.

rediscount

The discounting for a second time of a negotiable instrument, such as that done by a Federal Reserve bank for the benefit of a bank which originally discounted the instrument.

red tape

>A slang term meaning an excess of formal rules or procedures, often in the form of paperwork, which causes difficulties in getting a job done.

referee

>One who is appointed to hear and determine in a lawsuit or to aid and assist in bankruptcy proceedings.

reference

>A person or firm to whom inquiries may be directed to check on such information as the credit responsibility or character of an individual.

refunding

>The incurring of a new debt through the refinancing of an old one. The extension of payments on an old debt.

register, bond

>A book of original entry in which details about the purchase and sale of bonds for the firm's own investment account are recorded.

registered representative

>An expression in investments which refers to an employee of a member firm of a stock exchange who has been authorized to serve public customers of the firm.

registrar

>A person responsible for certifying to the public that stock issues are correctly stated and in accordance with the provisions of a corporation's charter.

reinstatement

> The right of an insurance policyholder, within a reasonable time after lapse, to reinstate his or her policy.

relational database

> A collection of organized data stored together and linked to one another according to various interrelated factors.

release

> A surrender by one party of the right to require a performance due from another party, or of the right of action arising from breach by the other party.

relief printing

> Letterpress printing in which the design to be reproduced is raised above the surrounding, non-printed area.

reminder letter

> A business letter, usually the first of a series of collection letters, sent by a creditor to a debtor who has not made a payment on time.

remittance

> The money paid on a debt. A payment on account. The act of sending money.

remote access

> The ability to communicate with a computer located some distance from the terminal.

rent

>A payment made periodically to an owner of property for the use of such property.

reorganization

>A major change in the organizational setup of a business firm either with respect to the capital structure or the interdepartmental relationships.

repayment

>The reimbursement of funds due or owed to a person or company.

replacement cost

>In insurance, this refers to the cost of restoration of property in the event of loss. In production and operations management, it is the cost of replacing broken or outdated equipment with new equipment.

replevin

>A legal suit instigated by a seller to regain possession of goods for which the buyer has failed to make the prescribed payments.

report

>To relate, state, write or provide notification of information, suggestions, or recommendations based on an investigation or study.

report, annual

>A report issued by a business firm at the end of a year's operation, showing the financial condition of the firm and the progress made since the last report.

report, cost

A report on findings related to costs of a business firm.

report, executive

A report compiled for top management.

report, progress

A report showing the progress made on a project or by a business firm over a stated period of time.

representative sample

A small group which is chosen to represent a population because of characteristics that closely match those of the population. Used in statistical analyses for prediction purposes.

reprint

To print again matter which has previously been printed.

requisition

A request in writing on a standard form that enumerates items to be ordered.

requisition, personnel

A request from a unit of an organization for workers needed to carry on assigned tasks.

requisition, purchasing

A formal request sent to the purchasing department, asking that an order be placed for enumerated items.

res

Property, a trust estate, or a trust fund.

research

Scientific investigation for the purpose of discovering new products or improved techniques.

research, market

The testing and investigation carried on in connection with everything and everybody concerned with the marketing function, such as packaging, pricing, the distribution system, the kind of person the consumer is, and the like.

research, public opinion

A study made as part of public relations to determine what the public thinks about a firm or about the firm's products.

reserve

In banking this term refers to that portion of deposits withheld from loanable funds in order to control the amount of money that can be credited through loans and to create a cushion to meet the withdrawal demands of depositors.

reserve, central bank

> The required deposits which a national bank must place with a Federal Reserve bank.

reserves, pyramided

> The process by which small county banks or state banks place part of their reserves with banks in nearby cities which, in turn, after holding out the required vault cash reserves, pass the deposits on until large amounts accumulate in the chief financial centers.

reserves, secondary

> That portion of deposit accounts which a bank sets aside or invests in high-quality, low-interest securities which can be converted into cash in a short period of time in an emergency.

resident buyer

> An agent, located in a major buying center such as New York, Chicago, or Los Angeles, who performs buying functions for a number of retailers. For example, the agent may buy merchandise, supply market information, analyze trends in styles and help on promotions. He or she is paid either a fee or a commission.

resignation

> The act of voluntarily giving up a job.

response time

> The average time that a computer takes to acknowledge a command or request from a user.

rest period

>A period allowed workers by a company in order to give them a chance to overcome fatigue, relieve monotony, and recharge their energy.

restraint of trade

>The action of a business firm or an agreement between two or more firms to try to prevent normal competition from functioning.

resume

>A summary. For example, a resume of a person is a summary of his or her history to date, and includes such information as education, business and personal background.

retail

>The sales at the ultimate consumer level. The final sale of one or several items, usually in small quantities, to be consumed by the purchaser.

retail advertising

>The advertising conducted by those selling to the ultimate consumer. Also, promotional selling by display.

retail chain

>A group of several retail stores under common ownership and management.

retail distribution

>The sale of goods or services through a retail outlet.

retailer

> A merchant who sells mainly to the ultimate consumer. Status as a retailer is established by customers as ultimate consumers rather than by the merchant's method of purchasing, size, or number of stores in the organization.

retainer

> A fee, usually to a consultant or a lawyer, placing that person on call to perform periodic services.

retention

> The amount held back. In some group insurance agreements, the retention is the amount of total premium the insurance carrier will keep, the rest to be paid in claims or to be refunded.

retirement

> The act of withdrawing from active employment because of age. Also the withdrawing from circulation as, for example, the retiring of currency.

retirement fund

> A trust fund established by a business organization and often contributed to by employees, used to provide a regular income for employees after they have retired from active work.

return on investment (ROI)

> The ratio of net profit to net worth. It is a widely accepted measure of management's ability to use capital productively.

roll-overs

> The practice of continually renewing short-term loans. If the pattern continues, it may be an indication of financial weakness or of expansion (growth).

ROM

> Acronyn for read only memory. Computer memory that contains permanently stored information that can be accessed at high speeds but cannot be altered by the user.

rotating internship

> A method of training whereby trainees of various sections of a business are interchanged periodically. This gives them an opportunity to become versatile and to develop an ability to adjust to new conditions.

rotating shift

> An arrangement whereby employees periodically change from the shift they are working to the next shift following.

round-table conference

> Any group meeting for discussion and interchange of ideas.

route sheet

> A written form used in the scheduling of production work.

routine

> A section of a program generally smaller than a module, which accomplishes a specific task.

routing

> In traffic management, this term is used to refer to the placing of orders for transportation service. In production, it refers to the scheduling of work. In sales management, it means the laying out of an itinerary for a salesperson. In office routine, it refers to scheduling of the flow of work or material.

rule of exceptions

> A guiding principle in good management which states that a responsible executive should be concerned with deviation from the norm in important matters rather than with routine work which can be delegated to subordinates.

run time

> The length of time required for a program to be fully executed.

S

sabotage

> As related to business affairs, this refers to the act by workers of purposely damaging or destroying the tools of production in plants where they work.

safety program

> A planned company program dealing with such matters as safety devices, potential hazards, first-aid instructions, and development of habits conducive to safety.

salary

> A fixed income or consideration for services paid on a weekly, monthy or annual basis as distinguished from a wage which is paid on an hourly basis.

sale

> A contract whereby the ownership of property is transferred from one person to another for some form of consideration.

sale, forced

> A sale which is made mandatory by action of a creditor.

sale on approval

> A sale in which title remains with the seller until the buyer manifests his or her intention to buy.

sale or return

> A clause in a contract stipulating that ownership will pass to the buyer immediately upon delivery, but that he shall have an option to return the goods if they are not satisfactory.

sales budget

> An estimate into the future of the probable sales revenue and probable selling costs for a given period of time.

sales contest

> A contest offered to salespeople in which either money or merchandise is offered as a reward for accomplishing a predetermined sales performance.

sales convention

> A mass gathering to which salespeople and key supervisory, administrative, advertising, and promotion personnel of an organization are invited. The purpose is to stimulate salespeople, give them an opportunity to exchange ideas, generate loyalty and award them for performance.

sales curve

> The same as a demand curve. A graphic representation showing the quantities of a product that will be sold at various prices.

sales divison

    The department or division of a business firm directing selling activities.

sales force

    The aggregate of salespeople who work for a particular business firm.

sales forecast

    An estimate of dollar or unit sales for a specified future period.

sales letter

    A business letter designed to sell a product or service.

sales management

    The planning, directing, and controlling of a sales organization.

sales manager

    The executive who plans, directs, and controls the activities of salespeople.

sales pitch

    The main idea in a sales presentation that is intended to convince the prospective customer to buy the product or service.

sales potential

    The total possible sales which a market can yield for any given period.

sales presentation

> The entire sales approach, including visual and verbal demonstrations, that is used when attempting to sell to a customer.

sales program

> An organized plan of selling which a business firm establishes in order to reach a predetermined sales goal.

sales promotion

> The coordination of advertising, publicity, personal salemanship, and customer services to promote profitable sales.

sales quota

> That share of a company's expected gross sales for a stated future period, apportioned to each district, branch office, territory and salesperson.

sales slip

> A written form, made out by the seller and presented to the purchaser, recording essential information about a sale.

sales talk

> A series of logically arranged, interrelated major ideas, so emphasized and illustrated as to arouse enthusiasm for, and have a tendency to engender action toward, the object intended.

sales tax

> Also called consumption tax. A tax imposed by state and local governments on goods and services purchased by ultimate consumers.

sales territory

>The district generally assigned to a salesperson. More generally, the geographical regions wherein selling and other related marketing functions take place.

sales volume

>The amount of sales made by a business firm during a given period.

salesmanship

>The art of selling. Skill in the presentation of goods and services for sale.

salesmen's floater

>A form of inland marine insurance which covers samples of merchandise as well as trunks and valises containing the samples.

saleswise

>A slang expression meaning a person who possesses sales knowledge or practices successful sales techniques.

salvaging

>The act of saving or of economically disposing of any parts of spoilage, waste or scrap which have further usefulness or value.

sampling

>The choosing of a moderately large group picked at random from a very large group in order to determine the characteristics of the large group from analysis of the smaller group.

sandwich criticism

In management, this is a method of evaluation where the manager will give criticism of unsatisfactory performance "sandwiched" between praise for the employee's good performance.

scab

Also, blackleg. A slang term for an employee who works during a strike.

scalar chain

The line of formal authority running from top to bottom of an organization.

scale

A progressive, graduated series. A graded system from the lowest to the highest.

scale, graphic

A representation depicting numerical information or comparisons by means of drawings or pictures.

scale, linear

A graphic representation using lines to depict numerical comparisons or information.

scalping

The act of buying and selling so as to make small, quick profits.

scarcity

> A lack or an insufficiency of a product or service to supply all levels of demand.

scatter chart

> A graph which has dots representing actual figures. Usually a line is added showing the average, trend or mean of the dotted array.

scatter diagram

> The pattern made by dots on a scatter chart.

scheduling

> The establishing of procedures for carrying out a process or project.

scrip

> Any temporary document which serves as a substitute for legal tender, entitling the holder to some article of value at some specified future time. Some industries in remote sections issue scrip to employees in order to diminish the amount of cash which would otherwise be required.

scrip dividend

> A written promise to pay in the future a dividend that has been declared by the board of directors of a corporation.

scroll

> To change text displayed on a computer screen by moving the cursor up or down, to the right or to the left.

seal of corporation

> A stamp, required by law, embossed on paper, used on important documents of a corporation.

sealed bids

> Secret written proposals or offers which are submitted by prospective suppliers before a certain date to a purchasing agent who has provided complete information regarding specifications and quantities required.

seasonal route

> A route over a territory traveled by salespeople from two to four times a year.

seasonal variation

> The month to month changes during the calendar year to which a particular kind of business is subject.

seat

> A term used to signify membership on a securities or commodity exchange.

secondary data

> Statistical or researched information which is based on indirect sources.

secondary distribution

> Also called secondary offering. A large block of stock, such as that which might be owned by an estate, which is redistributed after it has been initially issued.

secondary offering

> The same as secondary distribution. See definition of secondary distribution.

secondary storage

> Also called auxiliary storage. An additional storage unit that supplements the computer's primary storage. Such "backup" units are usually in the form of a disk or magnetic tape.

secretary

> An employee who attends to correspondence, filing and records.

secretary of corporation

> A paid executive officer who keeps the minutes of meetings of the board of directors and of stockholders, serves all notices of the corporation, is the custodian of the records and seal, and performs other important corporate duties.

section foreman

> A supervisor in manufacturing who is responsible for the work of other foremen and of their groups in his or her section.

secular trend

> A gradual long-term growth or decline in economic activity.

securities

> Stocks and bonds of business firms used to raise long-term capital.

Securities and Exchange Commission (SEC)

A government agency which has responsibility over the registration and sale of securities to the public.

security, employee

The degree to which an employee can rely on a job with no chance of layoffs or arbitrary dismissal.

security exchange

A place where stocks and bonds are bought, sold and traded.

seek time

The amount of time required for a disk drive to find a particular piece of data.

seigniorage

A charge, exceeding the actual cost of coinage, levied for coining bullion.

self-employed

A person who works for oneself, such as a sole proprietor, an independent consultant, a freelance writer or artist, etc.

self-insurance

An expression used to refer to the practice of some businesses of financing an insurance risk with their own resources rather than of paying premium to an insurance carrier.

seller

> A person who transfers services or title to property, receiving in exchange money or other valuable goods or services.

sellers' market

> The condition which exists when, under competitive conditions, the schedules of supply and demand are such that market prices are high, giving sellers an advantage. A time when demand exceeds supply, thus putting an upward pressuer on prices.

selling

> The personal or impersonal process of assisting or persuading a prospective customer to buy a commodity or service.

selling, door-to-door

> Selling to ultimate consumers at their place of residence.

selling, mail order

> Selling in which the order and delivery of goods is conducted by mail.

selling, retail

> Selling goods or services to the ultimate consumer as distinguished from selling to other buyers, such as to wholesalers or industrial concerns.

selling agent

> Also called a commission house. An independent business person or business operating on a commission whose principal function is to sell

the entire output of a manufacturer or of a limited number of manufacturers. Selling agents sell principally drugs, chemicals, paper, hardware and fabricated metals.

selling short

The same as short. See definition of short.

semiconductor

Synonymous with chip in popular usage. Technically, it is a chemical substance which, depending on a number of factors, can either conduct or not conduct electricity. Silicon is the most well known substance used for semiconductors.

semiskilled workers

Those employees whose jobs consist of routine duties requiring some training or ability, and a slight degree of decision-making.

senior security

A security such as a debenture or a preferred stock which has investment status and a relatively stable market because of its dependable fixed income and because of its prior position in the event of liquidation.

seniority

The status or rights secured by an employee for length of service with a company, usually for an unbroken period except for leaves of absence.

separation

The severance of a person from active employment in a firm.

serial

>Any device, or communications line, which moves data one bit at a time, one after another in a series.

serial printer

>An impact printing device that prints computer output one character at a time.

service, field

>A branch office established by a concern in order to provide repair service for company products in the locality where the consumer is located.

service, janitor

>The maintenance or clean-up service provided to a business organization.

service business

>A firm which provides services such as repairing as distinguished from one which provides products.

service department

>A department of a business which is engaged in repairing, restoring, inspecting, adjusting, or refueling items in order to make them fit for service.

services

>Intangibles such as acts of helpful activity or accomodations required by the public as distinguished from goods which are defined elsewhere.

servicing a bond

> Making the interest or pricipal payments on a bond on the due dates.

servomechanism

> A mechanical or electronic device such as a computer which, by means of instructions from a punched card or tape, gives instructions and directs the performance of an automated tool.

settlor

> In commercial law, this term is applied to a person creating a trust.

setup time

> The time required to prepare a machine tool for a particular job.

severance

> The termination of employment. The separation of oneself from work.

severance pay

> The pay received by an individual who has terminated his or her job with a business firm.

share

> A written document evidencing a fractional ownership in a corporation.

share warrant

> The right to purchase a given security at a fixed price, granted for a specified period of time.

shift

>The working hours which are put in by employees of a plant during a 24-hour period. The term is usually used where there is more than one shift, such as a day shift, a swing shift and a graveyard shift.

shift, day

>Plant working hours which generally extend from 7 A.M. to 3 P.M.

shift, graveyard

>Plant working hours which generally extend from 11 P.M. to 7 A.M.

shift, swing

>Plant working hours which generally extend from 3 P.M. to 11 P.M.

shift premium plan

>A method of paying workers in varying rates based on the particular hours of the day or night they work. For example, the graveyard shift between 11 P.M. and 7 A.M. may be paid more than the day shift.

shipping

>The preparing of finished stores for shipment to customers. The crating or marking of finished stores in preparation for sending them to customers.

shoe-string banking

>An abuse of banking in early days by which a person with, say $15,000, would organize a bank capitalized at $25,000, persuading others to invest $10,000. Having control, one would then borrow the original

$15,000 and use it to start another bank. Thus, with the original $15,000, one could start and control a chain of banks.

shop disciplinarian

The person in charge of discipline in a factory. He or she has the duty of building up confidence and cooperation between management and workers.

shop steward

The same as union steward. See definition of union steward.

shopping center, controlled

A trading location in which the owners of the project determine in advance the number and type of stores which will be permitted to have leases.

shopping goods

Those goods which are generally purchased with great care after comparison for service, quality, price, or style, as distinguished from convenience goods which are often bought on impulse.

short

A term used in investments to refer to the sale of stock which the seller does not yet own, but which he borrows from his broker in order to deliver it to the purchaser. He sells in the expectation that the stock price will decline and he can realize a profit because of the difference between his selling price and the price he pays for the stock.

short-term financing

The securing of funds which must be repaid within a short period of time, usually within a year.

SIC

    Abbreviation for standard industrial classification. A coding system for identifying companies within certain industries.

signature

    In advertising, this term refers to a company's trade mark or trade name on an advertisement or on a package.

signed advertisement

    An advertisement which has the name of the advertiser displayed, as distinguished from a blind advertisement which does not indicate the name of the advertiser.

silent partner

    See definition of partner, silent.

silk-screen printing

    A reproduction process in which the design is deposited on a surface or plate by forcing thick oil paint through a piece of silk cloth stretched over a frame. The parts of the silk not containing the design to be reproduced are treated so paint cannot ooze through them.

simo chart

    A graphic representation which shows the elements of an activity broken down into the time it takes for each element to be completed, used as a basis for production control.

simplex line

    A communications channel between computers which allows a single data transmission to be either sent or received, but not both. A simplex line is one directional as distinguished from a full duplex or half-duplex line which are both defined elsewhere.

single-line store

A retail store, such as a shoe store or men's clothing store, which specializes in a single kind of merchandise.

single proprietorship

The same as a sole proprietorship. See definition of sole proprietorship.

sinking fund

A fund in which periodic deposits are made for the purpose of paying a debt or of replacing an asset.

sinking fund reserve

An amount of earned surplus earmarked for redeeming or retiring an indebtedness, equal in amount to payments made in a sinking fund.

skilled workers

Those employees whose jobs require considerable training, expertise, and decision-making ability.

slogan

A group of words which, with constant repetition, will become associated with the goods or services of an advertiser.

smart terminal

A terminal with a significant amount of memory, and the capacity to do independent work, attached to a larger computer. Same as intelligent terminal.

Social Security

A national program of old age, survivors', disability and medical insurance benefits governed by the Social Security Administration according to the rules and regulations of the Social Security Act of 1935.

soft copy

Computer output that is displayed on a screen as distinguished from hard copy which is defined elsewhere.

software

All computer programs, including stored commands and procedures as well as pre-packaged application programs.

sole proprietor

A person who runs a sole proprietorship. See definition of sole proprietorship.

sole proprietorship

A business having a single owner who receives all the profits and who is personally liable for all debts the business may incur.

solicit

To appeal to an individual or to a group of prospects to buy something or to do something.

solicited reply

An inquiry or answer that is in response to an actual attempt to get such action.

solvent

> Being capable of paying debts. The condition which exists when assets exceed liabilities.

SOS

> Sophisticated Operating System. The operating system used by the Apple III computer.

source document

> Original data to be input to the computer.

source program

> A computer program written in a programming language that must first be converted to an object program before the computer will be able to run it.

space buying

> The purchase of advertising in printed media.

span of control

> The number of subordinates directed by a superior.

special event

> A promotion, such as a company tour or an open house sponsored or undertaken by a business.

special situations

> An expression in investments referring to stocks which appear to be a good short-term investment for reasons other than the normal ones. For

example, because of such things as a liquidation, receivership or reorganization, the stock of a company might be selling for less than its book value.

specialist

A term in investments referring to a broker on the floor of an exchange who executes limited orders and also buys and sells these securities for his or her own account.

special-trip route

An itinerary used by a salesperson for an emergency trip.

specialty goods

Products a customer is willing to make a special effort to acquire, such as specific brands of commodities with no acceptable substitutes.

specialty store

A retail outlet which handles products which are closely related, such as a jewelry store, a toy store, or a men's clothing store.

speculator

A person who is willing to assume a large risk in the hope that he or she can realize a relatively large gain.

spin-off

The distribution of the stock of a subsidiary company to the stockholders of a parent company.

split commission

The awarding of partial compensation to all salespersons who participate in making a sale.

split shift

> An arrangement of work hours in which the daily work is not continuous but is broken into two or more intermittent periods.

sponsored program

> A radio or television program which is paid for by an advertiser, as distinguished from a sustaining program.

spot announcement

> A radio or television commercial which is one minute or less in duration and which is usually repeated several times during the day.

spot field investigation

> A method of advertising research, usually used by small and medium sized advertisers, whereby primary research is conducted on a small scale in selected but scattered areas of distribution.

spot market

> A sale on the commodity exchange involving a cash transaction in which the buyer expects delivery of the commodity. The seller owns the commodity or has definite assurance of owning it, and ships it according to the directions of the buyer.

spot radio

> Radio programming which originates from a local radio station as distinguished from network programming.

spread

> In investments this term refers to the difference between the price an investment house pays for bonds and the price for which the bonds will be sold to the public.

square deal

    A slang expression meaning an honest, just business arrangement.

stabilization

    Act of making constant. For example the act of regulating the value of money in order to maintain its purchasing power at a constant rate.

stabilization, salary

    A policy designed to keep the income of salaried personnel at a constant level with as little fluctuation as possible.

stabilization, wage

    A policy designed to keep the income of wage earners at a constant level with as little fluctuation as possible.

staff

    A body of assistants who work to carry out the plans of their supervisor or manager.

staff assistant

    A specialist or consultant who aids in carrying out the plans of an operating manager.

staff function

    The giving of advice, service, or assistance in a business, as distinguished from the performance of work directly associated with the product.

standard

> A criterion established for a product either as to cost or specifications in manufacture, used as a basis for controlling the manufacture of future products of the same kind.

standard manufacture

> The production of goods or articles which conform to specified conditions established by the producer rather than the consumer. This distinguishes standard manufacture from customer manufacture which is the production of goods to meet customer specifications.

standard of living

> The level of comforts or luxuries in life to which a person or a group may be accustomed.

standardization

> The act of establishing and maintaining specific production criteria as to materials, weights, measurements, wearability and serviceability.

stand-by equipment

> Equipment owned by a company, representing production facilities beyond that normanlly used. Such equipment is available should an unusual peak load be created.

stand-by underwriting

> The practice of sellers, who specialize in the sale of new security issues, of purchasing during the subscription period any shares not bought by the buying public. The purpose is to maintain a price level until the shares are distributed.

state income tax

    A tax imposed by a state on the income of persons living or doing business within the boundaries of that state.

statement of account

    A monthly itemized statement sent to a credit customer of a business.

state of the art

    A term used to describe the very newest, or latest technological development in a given field.

statistical data

    An accumulation of numerical facts or figures that are assembled, classified, and tabulated so as to present significant information about a given subject.

statistical table

    A formal tabulation of research data from which the researcher can prepare illustrations, analyses and interpretations.

statistics

    The collecting, classifying, summarizing and interpreting of numerical facts. The term also applies to numerical facts themselves.

statutory law

    The written law which is adopted by the Congress of the United States or by the legislatures of the several states.

stencil

> A piece of thin sheet metal, parchment paper, or the like, perforated in such a manner that when it is laid on a surface and ink or color is applied, a pattern, design or printing is produced.

stereotypes

> Also known as "stereos." Printing plates used in the production of newspapers. The plates are cast from molten metal from a paper mold called a matrice.

sterilization of reserves

> Any method of eliminating bank reserves and rendering them ineffective as a basis for expanding bank loans and investments.

stock

> A share of ownership. Common and preferred shares issued by a corporation and representing ownership. Also a supply of materials maintained to meet the needs of production.

stock, authorized

> The number of shares authorized for sale in a corporation's charter.

stock, blue chip

> An expression used to refer to a relatively safe stock to invest in. A stock of a nationally-known corporation which has the reputation for making money and paying dividends in both good and bad periods.

stock, capital

> The same as stock. See definition of stock.

stock, convertible

> A preferred stock which under certain conditions can be exchanged for common stock.

stock, cumulative

> Preferred stock whose dividends are cumulative; that is, lapsed dividend payments of past periods must be made up before any action can be taken leading to a distribution of dividends to common stockholders.

stock, fully paid and nonassessable

> Capital stock which has been purchased from the company issuing it for the full par value. The cost of the stock represents the full extent of the owner's liability except perhaps for the liability of unpaid wages.

stock, issued

> The number of outstanding stock certificates of a company.

stock, low-par-value

> Low-par-value is a descriptive term rather than a particular kind of stock. It refers to stock with a relatively low stated value. Shares of such stock are sometimes issued to replace high priced shares. In such a case, the aggregate value of the new shares is equal to that of the old shares, but the stated value of a new share is lower, and there are more shares outstanding.

stock, noncumulative

> Preferred stock whose dividends are not cumulative; that is, if a dividend is not paid in a past period, it need not be made up before the board of directors takes action leading to a distribution of dividends to common stockholders.

stock, nonparticipating

> A preferred stock which is entitled only to the fixed rate of dividends stated on its face and to no more.

stock, nonvoting

> A type of stock, nearly always preferred stock, which does not give the holder the right to vote at stockholders' meetings of the corporation.

stock, no-par-value

> A stock certificate which bears no face value.

stock, participating

> A preferred stock which is entitled to share in the distribution of dividends beyond the fixed rate stated on its face.

stock, part-paid and assessable

> Capital stock which has been purchased from the company issuing it for less than the par value. The holder at any time can be assessed by the board of directors for the difference between the amount paid and the par value.

stock, par-value

> A share of stock with a stated value printed on the face of the certificate.

stock, treasury

> Capital stock which is issued and subsequently repurchased by a corporation.

stockholder

    A person owning a certificate or certificates of ownership in a corporation.

stop order

    A right of the Securities and Exchange Commission, granted by the Federal Securities Act of 1933, of delaying the sale of a securities issue at any time within a 20-day period from the registration if misleading statements are found in the registration statement. Also, an order authorizing a broker to buy or sell a stock at the market when it reaches a certain price.

stop payment

    The act of serving notice on a bank not to honor a check.

stopper, advertising

    Anything in advertising, such as color, which is used to attract the attention of a prospective customer.

storage

    Tape or disk drive where data can be stored. See primary storage, secondary storage or auxiliary storage.

storage unit

    A part of a digital computer in which is stored data to be remembered.

store

    A retail establishment where goods are offered for sale to ultimate consumers.

store, independent

> An establishment owned and operated as an individual unit as distinguished from a chain store. An organization with as many as three stores under one management can still be classified as an independent.

stores' credit slip

> An instrument of control used by the purchasing department for transferring responsibility for materials.

storing

> A function involving the warehousing and stocking of merchandise until it can be moved, in whole or in part, into the next channel in the stream of production and distribution.

straight commission

> A plan of compensation in sales whereby a salesperson is paid a percentage of his or her gross sales.

street certificates

> Securities which are kept in the name of a security investment house to facilitate delivery and transfer.

street name

> An expression referring to securities which are held in the name of a broker rather than the customer. It is called a street name because many brokers have a Wall Street address.

strike

> A concerted stoppage of work, slowdown, or interruption of operations by employees.

strike, jurisdictional

> A strike in which a union tries to get an employer to recognize its members rather than members of another union for stated types of work.

strike benefits

> Payments made by the union to its members while they are on strike and receiving no other compensation.

string

> A quantity of characters, numbers or signs that are usually handled by the computer as a unit. Each programming language has its own defined types of strings.

structural unemployment

> Unemployment caused by changes in population, technology, consumption or legislative policies, which are not directly related to the ups and downs of the business cycle.

stuffer

> An advertisement or piece of promotional literature placed in an envelope, such as a pay envelope, in addition to the main material.

stunts

> The use of unusual gimmicks or promotional ideas in order to attract attention to a company, its products or services.

subcontractor

> A person or firm contracting to perform specialized work for a contractor.

subordinate

An employee who is under the authority of another.

subrogation

The right of a second party who has settled the loss of a first party to receive all or part of the first party's right of indemnification from an injuring party.

subscriber

Someone who agrees or makes application to buy something. A person who agrees, usually in writing, to buy the stock of a corporation.

subscription agreement

A pre-incorporation agreement made by investors in a proposed new company to buy a specified number of shares if the corporation is chartered.

subscription date

The date on which propective investors in a new company must honor their promise to buy a specified number of shares.

subscription warrant

A printed certificate issued to a stockholder indicating the rights inherent in the stock he or she holds and the expiration date before which the rights must be exercised.

subsidiary

A company which is controlled by another organization called the parent company.

subsistence

A level of living providing only enough for one's own consumption needs.

subsistence allowance

The stated amount which a company will reimburse an employee for living expenses while engaged in affairs of business away from one's regular place of work.

suggestion box

A place in a business firm where employees are invited to deposit written suggestions or recommendations concerning any facet of the business operation.

suicide clause

A clause in a life insurance policy stating that if the insured commits suicide during a stated period of time after issuance of the policy, the company is not liable except for return of premiums.

summons

In law this term refers to a written order to a defendant to appear in court to answer a complaint or charges brought by a plaintiff.

superintendent

A person who is in charge of other employees in a department or a section of a business firm.

supervision

> The act of overseeing and inspecting with authority the work of employees who are on a lower managerial level. The exercise of a span of control over designated subordinates.

supervisor

> One who oversees and inspects with authority the work of subordinates.

supervisor, first-line

> A supervisor who is on the first or lower level of the management ladder.

supplier

> A business firm which provides commodities or services to another business firm.

supply

> The amount of commodities offered for sale at a given price at any given time.

supply curve

> A line on a chart which shows how the amount of a product or service which a producer will supply depends on the price one can get. Volume in increasing amounts is plotted on the horizontal axis of the chart. Price in increasing amounts is plotted on the vertical axis of the chart. Clearly, then, the line plotting the amount a producer will supply will start low on the chart when the price is low and will move upward as the price increases.

supply schedule

> The same as supply curve. See definition of supply curve.

supply side economics

> An economic theory based on the belief that lower tax rates will stimulate spending, which in turn will stimulate production (or, "supply"), which in turn will generate growth in the economy.

surety

> One legally liable for the debt, default, or failure of another. Also, security for payment or for the performance of some act.

surety bond

> A form of insurance protection which guarantees the performance of an act such as the construction of a building.

suretyship

> The relationship between the surety, the debtor, and the creditor. See definition of surety.

surplus

> The amount by which the assets exceed the liabilities and capital stock of an enterprise.

surplus, appropriated

> A part of surplus earmarked for specified purposes.

surplus, capital-reduction

    The adding to surplus an amount by which the par or stated value of stock has been reduced by an amendment of a company's charter. This increase in surplus allows management wider discretion in distributing dividends or in debiting sums against surplus.

surplus, paid-in

    Contributions to corporate capital that do not form a part of the legal or stated capital. Such surplus arises from transactions such as the sale of shares in excess of their par, stock assessments, and capital increases resulting from dealings in treasury stock.

survey

    A critical examination or study, relying on questions, in order to obtain knowledge or information about a subject.

survey, attitude

    A study to determine the opinions or feelings of the general public or of a particular public about a company, a product, or a service.

survivors' benefits

    See definition under old age and survivors' benefits.

sustaining program

    A radio or television program which is not sponsored.

sweat shop

    A slang term referring to a manufacturing operation which grossly overworks and underpays its employees, in order to make the highest possible profits.

swing route

>An itinerary used by salespeople who work in a comparatively restricted territory and who regularly visit their limited list of prospects and customers.

switchboard

>An apparatus consisting of a panel of switches from which the telephone communications of a business are combined, controlled, measured and protected.

switching and terminal services

>Services provided by a railroad, usually at a terminal, including switching, furnishing track and facilities (stations, elevators, warehouses, stockyards), and operating bridges and ferries.

symbolic program

>Same as a source program. See source program.

synchronous communication

>A method of data transmission in which two computers or other devices have their internal clocks in such harmony that they can send and receive data at times so preisely that the other device will always know exactly when to expect it, allowing for very high rates of transmission. See also asynchronous communication.

syndicate

>An association of persons, business, or banks, combined to carry out an undertaking requiring a large amount of capital, such as the underwriting of an issue of bonds.

syndicate, picture

    A business concern which sells photographs to the press for simultaneous publication in a number of newspapers.

syntax

    The grammar of a specific computer programming language. Using incorrect grammar, i.e. statements, commands or requests that the computer cannot understand, will result in a "syntax error."

system

    The data, hardware, software, personnel and money required to run a particular business or specific business function.

systems analyst

    A person, usually a computer specialist, who is responsible for analyzing existing business procedures and recommending changes—or new designs to improve the efficiency of the system.

systems software

    The programs written into the computer system that make it function. Operations covered by systems software include the operating system, utility functions which perform file handling, input-output controls, translation from source program to object program via compilers, interpreters and/or assemblers, etc. Systems software is distinguished from application software which is defined elsewhere.

T

tag board

    A heavy paper used for file folders and identification tags.

tally sheet

    A form designed to tabulate data obtained from a research project.

target market

    The segment of a market toward which the promotion is aimed.

tariff

    In transportaion, this term refers to the published rates and charges made by common carriers. Also, any tax on goods and services transported between nations.

task force

    Also, task group. A team of persons with a specific job to accomplish.

tax

    A compulsory contribution of a portion of a citizen's wealth for the support of the local, state, or federal government.

tax, capital gains

A tax levied by the federal government on profits realized from the purchase and sale of capital assets such as stocks.

tax, consumption

The same as a sales tax. See definition of sales tax.

tax, entrance

The charge levied on a foreign corporation wishing to do business within a state.

tax, estate

The same as an inheritance tax. See definition of tax, inheritance.

tax, excise

A duty levied on the manufacture, sale or consumption of certain goods within the country.

tax, federal income

A graduated tax exacted by the federal government on the annual income of individuals.

tax, franchise

A duty levied on the amount of outstanding or of authorized capital stock of a domestic corporation.

tax, inheritance

A tax on the net estate of a decedent's property, imposed by the state and federal governments.

tax, organization

> A duty levied on a corporation at the time it secures a state charter.

tax, privilege

> A duty levied on a foreign corporation based on the amount of stock owned by residents of the state or on the value of the company's assets within the state.

tax, proportional

> A duty levied at a constant rate regardless of the size of the tax base.

tax, regressive

> A duty levied at a decreasing rate as the tax base increases in size.

tax, regulatory

> A duty levied on occupations and products primarily to regulate rather than to raise revenue.

tax, severance

> A duty levied on the owner of forests or mines when the timber is cut or the minerals are removed.

tax, transfer

> Usually called stock transfer tax. See definition of stock transfer tax.

tax, use

> A state sales tax levied on goods entering the state from another state.

tax, withholding

> Tax money withheld from an employee's earnings and retained by the employer for the purpose of remitting it to the federal government.

tax adjustment

> A change in the tax levy imposed to raise or lower revenue to a needed level.

tax bracket

> The rate at which a levy is imposed on a person's income because of the level of one's taxable income. Personal income becomes taxed at progressively higher rates, an application of the principle of taxing on one's ability to pay.

tax loss carryover

> A loss of profit which for tax purposes can be readily applied against taxable earnings in subsequent years.

taxation

> The sovereign power of government enabling it to raise revenue for public purposes by means of forced contributions levied against income, property, use of facilities, and the like.

taxes, stamp

> A form of excise tax which is levied by means of selling stamps to affix on the product. For example, tobacco and alcohol are usually sold subject to stamp taxes.

teacher's kit

> Materials of assistance to teachers, prepared for distribution by a business organization for public relations purposes.

team player

> In management, a person who is cooperative when working with a group of fellow employees toward a common goal.

technical analysis

> In investments this expression refers to a method of evaluating stocks or bonds by studying market performance, as distinguished from fundamental analysis which is defined elsewhere.

technique

> The use of expert methods in accomplishing something in a particular field, such as the developed procedures used by a salesperson in closing a sale.

technology

> The science of knowledge of industrial arts, especially of the more important manufacturing processes such as spinning, weaving, metallurgy, extrusion and fabricating.

telecom

> Short for telecommunications; transmitting data, voice, video or any other type of information across distances.

telecommunication

> The transferrence of ideas and information between distant points by voice, signs, signals, writings, images, and sounds of any nature by wire, wireless, radio, television, or other systems of electrical or visual signaling.

teleconferencing

> Using computers and other electronic components to hold a meeting across distances.

telemarketing

> The process of doing direct marketing contact with potential customers by telephone. A list of telephone numbers is given to a caller who then proceeds to dial each individual with the intent of selling a product or service. Similar in concept to direct mail marketing, except by telephone instead of by postage.

telephoto

> A photograph taken with a combination of lenses designed to give a large image of a distant object in a camera of relatively short focal length.

teleprocessing

> Sending data to be processed (or receiving processed data) via standard telephone lines.

teletext

> A one-way transmission of messages, including graphics, to a remote video display screen. Teletext is distinguished from videotex which is defined elsewhere.

tight money

> An expression used by business men and economists to describe a situation resulting from a scarce supply of money or from some restrictive monetary policy used by the government in an effort to promote stability in the price level.

time-and-motion study

> A detailed analysis of a labor operation, broken into elemental components. Each movement is studied and the time of it is recorded. The purpose is to use the analysis to increase efficiency and to improve work habits.

time buying

> Purchasing goods to be paid for in installment payments. Also, the purchase of radio or of television time for advertising purposes.

time deposit

> Also called a savings account. A type of bank account which draws interest and which is not subject to withdrawal, except at the discretion of the bank, until after a 30-day notice is given to the bank by the depositor.

time series

> In statistics, this term refers to a table with numerical data classified chronologically.

time study

> An accurate determination of the time required to perform an operation by an employee. The time is then compared to a standard.

timekeeping

> An accounting function which consists of collecting basic payroll information, such as provided by time tickets or clock cards, in order that the accounting department can calculate the wages due each employee at the end of the pay period.

timesharing

> The use by business of large mainframe computers, owned by other companies, in sometimes distant locations. Also, a method of sharing central processor time between terminals.

title

> The exclusive rights, powers, privileges, and immunities to property, real and personal, tangible and intangible, possessed by the holder or holders against all other persons.

title, absolute

> A legal instrument, indicating the unqualified right of ownership of personal or real property.

tolerance

> The limits of permissible inaccuracy above and below specification in the fabrication of an article.

tool and equipment section

> The department responsible for the issuance, maintenance, and safekeeping of hand tools and large equipment.

tooling

> The act of preparing, assembling, and setting up the tools necessary to perform one or more operations in manufacturing a product.

top executive

A member of the top level of management of a business firm.

top management

The policy-making directors and senior managers of a business firm. The top executives of an organization.

tort

A moral wrong or a private wrong which a person does, causing damage or loss to another. For example, threats, libelous statements, and inducing another to break a contract are common examples of torts.

track

A concentric circle on a computer disk used as a location for storing and accessing data. Tracks are magnetic, not physically grooved.

trade acceptance

A time draft drawn by the seller of goods for the purchase price of goods, accepted by the buyer and payable on a certain date and at a certain place.

trade association

An association of kindred business firms, formed for the purpose of mutual interest or the exchange of information.

trade channel

The method by which a company's product gets to the consumer. The middlemen through whom title passes from producer to final consumer.

trade discount

A monetary allowance given by a business firm in recognition of the function of the receiver.

trade discount, functional

A monetary allowance made on the basis of classifications of buyers. The price differential is made on the basis of the function involved regardless of quantities purchased.

trade discount, pure

A monetary allowance which serves the purpose of preventing comparisons by different buyers and hence serves to conceal the actual net price charged various customers. Such discrimination is now generally forbidden by law.

trade journal

A magazine devoted to the interests of a specific trade, business, or industry.

trademark

A legally protected mark, symbol or design which is affixed to a product in order to distinguish it from others.

trade name

The same as brand name. See definition of brand name.

trade secret

Information kept from the general public or from competitors about the identity of a product, its components, or the nature of its manufacture.

trade show

>An exhibition or public display where merchandise of a particular industry is shown to customers or persons engaged in the same trade.

trade union

>A labor union composed of workers engaged in a particular craft.

trader

>A merchant engaged in trade or commerce who makes a business of buying, selling, or barter. A member of the stock exchange, trading for oneself and not as an agent for customers.

trading area

>A district whose boundaries are usually determined by the economical buying or selling which can be accomplished from a given point of distribution.

trading on the equity

>An expression meaning the same as leverage. See definition of leverage.

trading posts

>The central locations in a stock exchange where buying and selling are conducted by members of the exchange.

trading range

>A price range at which investors and speculators can afford to purchase a reasonable number of shares of a security.

traffic

>The movement of persons or goods. Also, the potential customers who frequent a business firm.

traffic control

>In a business firm, the regulation of vehicles, their routes, and the quantity of freight carried in a given period.

traffic density

>The volume of traffic moved by a particular kind of carrier. The formula is $F.T.D. = T.M./M$ in which $F.T.D.$ is freight traffic density, $T.M.$ is ton miles, and M is mileage of line.

traffic manager

>The person who administers traffic functions, directs the receiving, packing, and shipping rooms, and supervises the motor-truck fleet, the warehouses, and other service facilities.

traffic stopper

>A point-of-purchase display or advertisement used to attract prospective buyers.

training

>The process of teaching an employee the information or skills one needs to carry out one's job or task effectively.

training, formal

>Instruction of employees through the use of manuals, discussions, lectures, films, courses, classes, conferences, and the like.

training, informal

>A process of instructing employees by showing them how to do an actual job and by giving them counsel and encouragement.

training, on-the-job

>The instruction of an employee in an actual job or task by an instructor experienced in the work.

transaction-oriented processing

>The processing of data at the time that it is entered into the computer system. Input can take place at the computer itself or at a remote terminal.

transcribed program

>A radio or television show which is transmitted electronically on a record-like disk, sound-tape, wire recorder, or video-tape device.

transfer

>The shifting of an employee from one position to another or from one department to another.

transfer, lateral

>The shifting of an employee from one position to another without increasing his or her duties, reponsibilities, requirements, or pay.

transfer agent

>The individual or corporate agency which maintains the ownership records of a corporation and makes the transfer of title to corporate securities. This duty is often performed by the trust department of a bank.

transfer and inheritance tax

A tax which is imposed on property which changes hands as a result of death.

transistor

A single semiconductor circuit. Chips often consist of more than 60,000 transistors.

transit

The causing to pass or be conveyed as "transit of goods." Also, a telescopic instrument mounted on a tripod used to establish lines and to measure angles in surveying.

translator

A type of program used to convert a source program into an object program. See also assembler, compiler and interpreter.

trans-lux

A magnified ticker tape which is projected on a wall or some prominent place where customers and investors can readily see it. See definition of Ticker tape.

transportation

The movement of goods from the points where they are produced or processed to other points where they are manufactured, distributed, stored, or consumed.

transportation, pipeline

A form of transportation in which liquids, gases, and some solids are moved through pipes from one point to another.

transportation floater

A form of inland marine insurance which supplements marine insurance by giving protection to property while it is being transported by rail, air, truck and steamer.

transposition

An error in record keeping, caused by reversing the digits in an amount when copying it or entering it in a machine.

traveler's check

A draft payable on sight, issued by a bank, express company or travel agent to a traveler who signs the document once when it is purchased and again when it is cashed.

treasurer

An executive of a business corporation who directs its finances. He or she controls revenue, authorizes expenditures, keeps financial records, and makes reports to the president and the board of directors.

treasury currency

Currency issued by the U.S. Treasury Department.

treasury stock

Stock which has been issued by a corporation and subsequently reacquired by it.

trend

The general movement of something, such as commodity prices or power consumption, in a particular direction over a period of time.

trial balance

> The listing of all accounts into a schedule form to make sure they balance as the first step in the preparation of financial statements.

troubleshooting

> A management activity of looking for and eliminating problematic situations.

trust

> Property which has legally been placed at the disposal of designated persons to be administered, invested or held for the benefit of a third party or parties. A plan whereby the voting rights of a majority of two or more corporations are assigned to trustees who then direct the affairs of the corporation. Also, any large corporation or combination of corporations exercising monopoly power in an industry.

trust company

> A form of bank authorized by state law to serve as trustee of funds and states. Trust companies also perform other services for business firms, such as acting as registrars or transfer agents.

trust fund

> Property which is legally placed in the hands of a trustee to be maintained for the benefit of a third party. Money, securities and other property held in trust.

trust fund, common

> The pooling together of trust money from several estates in order to purchase securities.

trust receipt

> In banking this term refers to a method of getting a loan by using merchandise as collateral. The borrower agrees to hold the commodities in good condition, subject to the order of the bank, until the terms of the agreement are fulfilled. Title remains with the bank. The bank is protected through a trust receipt.

trustee

> A person who receives legal title to property and manages it for another.

trusteed pension plan

> A retirement plan whereby money is placed in a trust fund where it accumulates tax free for employees.

turnaround document

> A computer produced form that can also be used as input. For example, a bill in the form of a punched card can be used as input to the computer (i.e. recording payment of the bill when returned by the customer).

turnaround time

> The time it takes between submitting a job to a computer center and receiving the results.

turnkey system

> All the hardware and software necessary in a complete computer system that can be installed as a unit. The user has only to turn the machine on in order for it to be usable, hence the name "turnkey system."

turnover

> The number of times a complete stock of goods is sold in a given period. Also, the change in personnel over a period of time as the result of those who terminate employment being replaced by others.

two-price house

> A business which sells merchandise or services to the same kinds of customers at different prices.

Type A personality

> Based upon a medical analysis of busy executives, the typical Type A personality is someone who is harried, high strung, impatient, eager to achieve, and in general, tends to push too hard for success. Such a personality type carries with it a record of high achievement but also the potential for serious health problems, such as heart or vascular concerns.

typography

> The art of printing. Also, typesetting or the arrangement of parts in a piece of type composition.

U

ultra vires act

    An act by a corporation's agents, officers, or directors, exceeding the rights of the charter. An act of this type is usually void.

undercapitalized

    A business whose capital structure is insufficient for effective operation.

under the table

    The same as off the books. See definition of off the books.

underwriter

    One who guarantees the sale of securities. Also, an investment bank which purchases securities for public distribution. Also, an insurance specialist who examines an application for an insurance policy and determines whether or not one's company should assume the risk.

underwriting

    The act by investment bankers of purchasing shares of stock for public distribution. Also, the act of guaranteeing the sale of securities or the assumption of a risk by an insurance company.

underwriting syndicate

    The same as syndicate. See definition of syndicate.

unemployment

    The act of being out of productive work for which one is paid. The state of not having a regular paying job.

unemployment, chronic

    A condition of continuing and persistent unemployment.

unemployment, cyclical

    The type of unemployment caused by a deflationary phase of a business cycle.

unemployment, frictional

    The type of unemployment which exists when a person has quit a job for reasons of one's own and has not yet secured another job but is in search of one.

unemployment, seasonal

    The type of unemployment caused by the seasonal variations inherent in a business or an industry.

unemployment, technological

    The type of unemployment resulting from machines replacing manpower, from the innovation of new techniques, or from retooling.

unemployment, voluntary

> The type of unemployment which exists when an employee has resigned from a job and refrains from accepting another.

unemployment compensation

> An income, usually paid weekly, to workers who are both willing and able to work but who are unable to get a job. A program sponsored by the U.S. government under the Federal Social Security Act of 1935 which assists the states in providing compensation for the unemployed.

unfair trade laws

> State laws which establish minimum price levels below which goods cannot be sold at retail.

uniform commercial code (UCC)

> In the U.S., the group of laws that governs commercial transactions between all of the states except Louisiana.

union

> An association of workers, according to crafts, trades, or both, formed for the purpose of improving the welfare of the workers through control of the size of the membership and through improved bargaining ability with business firms.

union, company

> An independent association of workers, organized and operating in one particular business firm.

union, craft

A labor organization composed of workers of a particular skill or trade or of several skills or trades. A trade union, a guild.

union, industrial

A union composed of workers in the same industry, such as steel workers, clothing workers, or automobile workers.

union, trade

The same as a craft union. See definition of union, craft.

union recognition

A situation where an employer admits the right of employees to choose their own representatives and agrees to recognize the chosen union as the bargaining agent for the workers.

union shop

A company which can employ non-union workers but all workers must join the union after a prescribed period and must remain in good standing with the union as a requirement of continued employment.

union steward

A worker who officially represents members of a union in their complaints and grievances with the management of a company. He or she is appointed to this job by the union.

unit cost

The cost of one article or unit of production.

UNIVAC

> The first commercial computer, built in 1951.

universal product code (UPC)

> A bar code that is printed on many consumer items and can be read by a scanning device as direct input to a computer system.

universe

> A term used in research to describe the total market or area under investigation, of which usually only a resentative sample is studied.

unsecured loan

> A loan supported by the general credit of the debtor rather than by collateral.

unskilled workers

> Those employees who hold jobs that are mostly repetitious, and require little or no formal training.

user-friendly

> A term used to describe ease-of-use of a computer program or system.

usury

> The charging of interest rates on loans in excess of the maximum rate permitted by statute.

usury laws

> An expression used in referring to state laws which stipulate the maximum rates of interest which can be charged on different types of loans.

utility program

> Software that provides file handling functions such as sorting, merge, format, or copy. Utility programs can be part of the systems software or part of an application package.

V

vacation

> A prescribed period of exemption from work granted to employees for rest or recreation.

valuation

> The act of estimating the worth of property according to some recognized criteria.

value

> The worth of a good or service. The quantity of one thing, especially money, that will be given in exchange for another thing.

value, replacement

> The amount of money necessary to restore an asset to its original worth or to replace an asset that has been lost.

value-added carrier

> A telecommunications company that offers communications channels with extra features that they charge more for.

variable

>A measure of dispersion of a frequency distribution.

variety store

>A retail store, originally known as a 5 and 10 cents store, which sells primarily convenience goods. Because such goods are generally bought on impulse, the store is located in a heavy traffic center such as on a main street in a downtown area or in the heart of a suburban shopping center.

vari-type

>A typewriter with interchangeable type, useful where a distinctive face of type is required, such as in the preparation of bulletins, special reports, and advertising material.

VCR

>Abbreviation for video cassette recorder.

vending machine

>A mechanical coin operated device which dispenses various types of commodities to the ultimate consumer such as cigarettes, soft drinks, candy, coffee, gum, etc.

vendor

>A supplier or a selling organization.

vendor's record

>A file on suppliers maintained by a purchasing agent.

venture capital

>Money or property which is invested at considerable risk to develop a new product or business. Money used to start a new business enterprise. Any investment in the ownership of an enterprise.

vertical integration

>Expansion of an industrial enterprise toward the objective of controlling all, or some major part, of the progressive stages from the time a product starts as a raw material until it arrives in the hands of the ultimate consumer.

vested

>Pertaining to the rights which go along with absolute ownership.

vested interest

>An established claim to real or personal property. Also, the property-owning, moneyed class of society.

vestibule training

>Training of an employee at a place away from the job but under conditions which are similar as much as possible to the job situation.

vice president

>The title of an executive who ranks next in command under a president and who usually is in charge of one segment of a business operation, such as marketing, production, or finance.

videotex

A two-way transmission system where users can send and receive data. One of the uses of this medium is sales of merchandise to videotex subscribers who can order items shown to them on a video display screen by keying information to the videotex company on a keyboard.

vocational training

A training program for a particular trade or skill.

voice recognition unit (VRU)

A device that interprets voice signals and transmits them as input into a computer.

voting, cumulative

The casting of as many votes as equal the number of shares possessed by a stockholder, multiplied by the number of directors to be elected. The voter may concentrate all the votes on one candidate, or divide the votes between two or more candidates.

voting by proxy

Casting a vote for another. See definition of proxy.

voting trust

A type of business combination wherein the voting stock of business firms is deposited in the hands of trustees to be voted as a unit.

voucher

A written form used in the operation of the voucher system. There are a number of vouchers, such as purchase voucher, cash voucher, petty cash voucher, and payroll voucher.

voucher system

A method of accounting control based on approvals of all aspects of each business transaction. This is effected by the use of vouchers authorizing each entry and disbursement.

wage

> The price paid for the services of a worker.

wage, average

> The arithmetical mean of the total wages paid any particular group.

wage, guaranteed annual

> An amount of pay guaranteed a worker by contract for each week of the year or for 48 weeks, regardless of the changes in the financial condition of the business firm.

wage, money

> The actual dollars and cents an employee receives as compensation for services rendered as distinguished from real wage.

wage, real

> The amount of foods and services a wage will buy for an employee as distinguished from money wage.

wage, time

The wage paid an employee based on the amount of time he or she works, such as per hour, week or month. Accurate records are often maintained for the payment of time wages through the use of time cards and time clocks.

wage incentive

Added compensation used to stimulate workers to strive for exceptional performance in their work.

wages, indirect

Fringe benefits. Monetary considerations other than regular wages, such as paid vacations, sickness and health benefits, and profit sharing. This expression is also used at times to mean indirect labor. See definition of indirect labor.

wagon distributor

Also called wagon jobber. A wholesaler who operates small warehouses and carries merchandise to retail customers in trucks (formerly wagons).

wagon jobber

The same as wagon distributor. See definition of wagon distributor.

waiver

The excusing of a performance. For example, an insurance premium may be waived in the event of total disability.

waiver of notice form

> A form, signed by incorporators after the certificate of incorporation is filed, which excuses the prior announcement of the first directors' meeting and consents to hold it immediately.

walkout

> A strike which is unauthorized by a union. The term is sometimes used as a synonym for a strike. See definition of strike.

warehouse

> A place for storage used for holding merchandise until needed for future use.

warehouse, receipt

> A certificate issued by a warehouse to a person, containing a description of goods stored in it. Such a receipt is sometimes used as a negotiable instrument.

warehousing

> The business of keeping merchandise in a storehouse until needed for further use.

warehousing, field

> A system of warehousing in which the warehouse goes to the goods rather than vice-versa. The goods are stored on the premises of the manufacturer or distributor in a fenced-off place, and the warehouse acts as custodian tending to proper receipt and release of goods.

warrant

> The same as stock warrant. See definition of stock warrant.

warranty

    A legal promise by a seller that property is or will be as represented.

warranty, express

    A statement by a seller, testifying that the goods one is selling have certain guaranteed characteristics.

warranty, implied

    The assumption that a seller of goods has a clear title to them, and that the goods will be usable for the purpose for which they were bought.

wasting-asset corporation

    A company whose assets dwindle, such as a mining company.

watered stock

    Stock issued for overvalued property or services.

wealth

    Material objects owned by people, inherently useful and relatively scarce. The sum total of things owned which have a money value.

wealth, economic

    Things which are scarce and are measured in terms of money.

wealth, private

    Wealth owned by individuals, whether they be persons or businesses as distinguished from public wealth or the aggregate of the nation's wealth.

wealth, social

> The sum total of wealth which is both free and economic. Free wealth means things which are neither scarce nor measured in terms of money, such as fresh air or sunshine. Economic wealth is defined elsewhere.

weighted average

> The average of a series of numbers which have been assigned a weight or value in order to allot to each of them its true importance in relation to the others.

welfare fund

> A benefit, set aside for employees or their families, which will be paid at some future date if certain predetermined circumstances come about.

welfare

> A U.S. government system of public programs to provide assistance to needy persons, including the elderly, disabled, handicapped, poor, and families with dependent children. Welfare assistance can take the form of monetary payments, food coupons, free or reduced medical, housing or educational costs, and the like.

whistleblower

> A slang term for an employee who, against the will of his or her employers, tells the public about a company activity perceived to be harmful, dangerous, morally wrong, etc.

white collar worker

> An employee whose job is mostly administrative or clerical, rather than production-oriented. Office workers are referred to as white collar workers.

white space

In advertising this expression refers to those parts of an advertisement where type and reproductions do not appear.

wholesale

The selling of large quantities of goods through a middleman for resale.

wholesale merchant

One whose business is to sell goods in large quantities to retailers.

wholesaler

A middleman who sells merchandise to cash retailers and other dealers who pick up the goods at his or her place of business.

wholesaler, limited-function

A merchant middleman such as a rack jobber who does not provide the full services of a wholesaler.

wholesaler, specialty

A middleman who carries a limited line of goods within a particular field.

wholesaler, voluntary-chain

A voluntary association of retail merchants banded together to perform joint merchandising and advertising functions. Such a wholesaler operates chiefly in the food, drug and hardware fields.

wildcat strike

>A strike by union members, unauthorized by union leaders, and usually in violation of the union contract.

winding up

>The process of settling the accounts and liquidating the assets of partnership or corporation for the purpose of making distribution and of dissolving the concern.

wiped out

>A slang expression referring to the complete loss of business or property because of reverses or an act of God.

wire fate items

>An expression used in banking to refer to notes sent for collection to out-of-town banks, accompanied by instructions to notify the sending bank by wire whether or not the obligations are honored.

wire service

>A news gathering organization which feeds national news to clients such as newspapers, radio and television stations.

wire transfer

>A term describing the means by which funds are transferred from one bank to another.

word processing

>Keying text into a computer that has software programmed for manipulation of the words and sentences, and whole paragraphs. Includes printing of text and documents.

workaholic

> A person whose work habits are excessive to the point of interfering with that person's physical health, interpersonal relationships and social functioning.

work hours

> The daily time an employed person is expected to actively engaged in performing the duties of one's job.

work-in-process

> Material in any of the stages through which it passes in being made into a finished product.

work sheet

> The same as working sheet. See definition of working sheet.

work stoppage

> The halting of work by employees engaged in a labor-management controversy.

working capital

> The excess value of current assets of a company over the current liabilities.

working conditions

> The environment of a work place, including such things as the physical conditions, monetary compensation, hours of work, and personnel policies.

working sheet

> A printed form used in accounting on which accounts and adjustments are classified as a first step toward closing the books at the end of an accounting period.

write

> To record data on a computer disk or tape.

write-off

> The cancelling of an asset. The declaring of a former asset to be of no value.

written report

> A presentation of a subject in writing in an accurate, impersonal, and complete manner.

Y

yellow-dog contract

    An agreement not to join a union forced on a worker as a condition of employment. This was outlawed by the Norris-LaGuardia Act.

yield

    The return on bonds at a given price as computed from bond tables. The rate of income derived from a stock at the prevailing dividend rate, obtained by computing the percentage of the annual distribution to the price.

"you" attitude

    The approach in a business letter when the letter is written from the point of view of the reader rather than the writer in order to help motivate the reader to do what the writer wants him or her to do.

Z

zero-balance account

> A cash disbursement bank account that allows a company to retain funds in a central pool, cover checks presented and avoid overdrafts, all at the same time. Funds are transferred to the zero-balance account automatically to cover payments.

zero base budgeting

> A method of budgeting costs which requires managers to justify every cost, not just the increase or decrease in costs from a prior period.

zero base inventory

> An inventory management system, sometimes called stockless production, that provides inventory only at the time it is needed in the production process. This is in contrast to a stock of inventory that may not be needed immediately.

zero defects

> A production management objective based on the principle: Do the job right the first time.

zip code

    A five number code used in the United States to identify post offices and permit automated sorting of mail.

zip + 4

    The addition of four more numbers to a zip code to identify city blocks, individual buildings, rural routes, post office boxes and even firms and floors within buildings.

zone campaign

    A method of gradually achieving national advertising by advertising from territory to territory until advertising on a national scale is accomplished.

zoning

    The partition by a city, town or village by ordinance of its area into sections reserved for various uses such as industrial, commercial or residential.

Business Term Locator

Data Processing Terms

access time
accumulator
acoustic coupler
address code
ALGOL
alpha-numeric card code
ALU
analog computer
APL
application
application software
arithmetic unit
array
artificial intelligence
ASCII
assembler
assembly language
asynchronous communication
auxiliary storage

backup
band printer
bandwidth
bar code reader
BASIC
batch processing
baud
binary card code

binary coded decimal
binary digit
binary input
bit
black box
branching
bootstrap program
BPI
buffer
bug
bus
byte

CAD/CAM
centralized data processing
chaining
channel
chip
circuit
circuit board
clock rate
COBOL
code
coding
compatible
compiler
computing
continuous form

DATA PROCESSING TERMS

control unit
CP/M
CPU
CRT
cursor

daisywheel
data
data flow diagram
data processing
data processing, centralized
data processing, decentralized
data processing, distributed
database
database management system
debug
dedicated line
dedicated system
default
demodulation
digital
direct access
disk
disk drive
documentation
dot-matrix printer
download
downtime
dump
duplex line
drum printer

EBCDIC
EDP
electronic
electronic funds transfer (EFT)
electronic mail
electronic spreadsheet
ergonomics
execution

facsimile equipment
fiber optic cable

field
file
firmware
floppy disk
flowchart
font
footer
format
FORTRAN
full duplex line

graphics display terminal

hacker
half-duplex
hard copy output
hard disk
hardware
head
header
high level language
Hollerith code
housekeeping

IC
impact printer
information
initiation
input
intelligent terminal
interactive
interface
interpreter

joystick

keypunch

LAN (local area network)
laser printer
letter quality printer
light pen
line printer
log on
loop

DATA PROCESSING TERMS

machine, punch card
machine language
magnetic core storage
magnetic disk storage
magnetic drum storage
magnetic storage
magnetic tape input
mainframe
megabyte (MB)
memory
menu
MICR
microcomputer
microprocessor
minicomputer
mode
modem
modulation
module
monitor
mouse
MS-DOS
MTBF
multiplexer
multiprocessing
multiprogramming

nanosecond
network
node
nonimpact printer

OCR
object program
OEM
office automation
offline
online
operating system
operation
optical scanner
output
output unit

page printer
parallel interface
parity bit
parity check
PASCAL
PBX
PC-DOS
peripheral
picosecond
PLI
plotter
port
primary storage
prompt
program
protocol

query language

RAM
read
real time
record
relational database
remote access
response time
robotics
ROM
routine
run time

scroll
secondary storage
seek time
semiconductor
serial
serial printer
servomechanism
simplex time
smart terminal
soft copy
software
SOS

DATA PROCESSING TERMS

source document
source program
storage
storage unit
string
synchronous communication
symbolic program
syntax
system
systems analyst
systems software

telecom
teleconferencing
teleprocessing
teletext
timesharing
track
translator
transaction-oriented processing
transistor
turnaround document
turnaround time
turnkey system

UNIVAC
universal product code (UPC)
user-friendly
utility program

value-added carrier
videotex
voice recognition unit (VRU)

word processing
write

Financial Terms
ABC analysis
accelerated depreciation
acceleration clause
acceptance
acceptance, bank

acceptance, trade
accomodation paper
account
account, asset
account, capital
account, open-book
account, profit and loss
account, time deposit
account, zero-balance
account executive
accounting
accounting, accrual basis
accounting, cash basis of
accounting, cost
accounting, double entry
accounting, payroll
accounting, single entry
accounting department
accounting equation
accounting system
accounts, uncollectible and execution proof
accounts payable
accounts receivable
accrued expenses
accrued income
accumulated depreciation
acid test
across-the-board
adjustable rate mortgage
adjusting entries
adjustment
ad valorem duty
advance
advance commitment
after-acquired clause
aged receivables report
aging schedule
agio
allonge
allowance
all-savers certificate

FINANCIAL TERMS

amortization
arbitrage
arbitrager
arrangement
arrears
asked
asset
assets, current
assets, fixed
assets, frozen
assets, intangible
assumed obligation
assumption of a debt
attrition
audit
auditing
auditing department
auditor
authorized
averages
averaging down

balance sheet
balance sheet equation
balloon maturity
bank
bank, commercial
bank, correspondent
bank, investment
bank acceptance
bank balance
bank charge
bank credit
bank deposits
bank money
bank statement
bargain counter
base year analysis
bear
bear market
bearer
beta coefficient

bid
Big Board
Big Eight
bill of exchange
bill of lading, negotiable
bill of lading, order
bond
bond, accumulation
bond, assumed
bond, baby
bond, bankers' and brokers' blanket
bond, bearer
bond, collateral trust
bond, continued
bond, convertible
bond, cost
bond, coupon
bond, debenture
bond, divisional
bond, equipment trust
bond, guaranteed
bond, income
bond, mortgage
bond, premium
bond, profit sharing
bond, refunding
bond, registered
bond, revenue
bond, serial
bond, sinking fund
bond averages
bond discount
bond yields
bond yield to maturity
book value
bookkeeper
borrower
bottom line
bourse
break-even analysis
break-even chart
broker

407

FINANCIAL TERMS

brokerage
brokerage house
bucket shop
budget
budget, cash
budget account
budget department
budget variance
budgetary control
budgeting
bulge
bull
bull market
business trust
buy in
buying on margin
buy out
call
call money
call price
calls and puts
capital
capital, circulating
capital, fixed
capital, fluid
capital, quick
capital asset
capital budget
capital expenditure
capital gain
capital gains tax
capital investment
capital structure
capitalization
capitalize
cash budget
cash cycle
cash flow
cash forecasting
cash receipts
cashier's check
certificate of deposit (CD)

certified check
certified public accountant
CFO
charge-offs
check
check register
chief financial officer
clearing house
close, the
closed-end investment trust
closing
collateral
co-maker
combined statement
commercial paper
commercial paper house
commission
commitment fee
common stock
compensating balance
comptroller, controller
consolidation
consumer finance
contingent liability
contribution margin
conversion parity
corner-the-market
corporation income tax
correspondent bank
cost-benefit analysis
cost control, accounting
cost control, operational
cost of capital
cost of goods sold
costs, direct
costs, historical
costs, indirect
costs, standard
coupon
C.P.A.
creative financing
credit

credit, documentary
credit, intermediate
credit line
creditor, general
creditor, preferred
cum pf

date of record
debenture
debt
deferred asset
deferred charge
deferred credit
deferred income
deferred liability
deficit
deficit financing
demand deposit
depository bank
depreciation
depreciation, double declining balance
depreciation, straight-line
depreciation, sum-of-the-digits
depreciation, unit production
depreciation, working hours
desterilization of reserves
development credit corporation
discount, bank
discounted cash flow methods
diversification
dividend
dividend, cumulative
dividend, patronage
dividend, stock
dollar cost averaging
double-name paper
double taxation
Dow Jones average
draft
draft, bank
draft, commercial

draft, sight
draft, time
drawee
drawer
due date
due presentment
duties, compound
duties, specific
duty

earned surplus
earning power
earnings
earnings, retained
eligible paper
endorsement
endorsement, blank
endorsement, conditional
endorsement, qualified
endorsement, restrictive
endorsement, special
endorser, accomodation
equity
equity capital
excess profits tax
exchange, stock
ex-dividend
expense
expense, administrative
expense, entertainment
expense, general
expense, operating
expense, selling
expense account
Export-Import Bank (Eximbank)
ex-rights

face value
factor
factoring
factoring company
Fannie Mae
F.A.S.B.

FINANCIAL TERMS

Federal Home Loan Mortgage
   Corporation
Federal National Mortgage Association
Federal Reserve System
FIFO
finance
finance bill
financial management
financial ratios
financial statements
financier
financing, short-term
financing, wholesale
financing plan, retail
fiscal
fiscal agent
fiscal policy
fiscal year
fixed capital
fixed rate mortgage
float
floating interest
floor
formula investing
Freddie Mac
funds
funds statement
futures
futures market

gilt-edge
goldsmith's note
greenbacks
gross margin
gross profit
group banking
growth stock

hidden asset
holder in due course
honor
hypothecate
hypothecated account

IOU
in the black
in the money
in the red
income
income statement
insolvent
installment buying
installment plan
installment selling
institutional investor
interest
interest, accrued
interest, compound
interest, effective rate of
interest, nominal rate of
interest, simple
internal audit
internal rate of return
investment banking
investment company
investment house
investment tax credit
investment trust
investor
IRR
issue price

job cost system
journal
journal, cash disbursements

lease
leasing asset
ledger
ledger, stock
lending institution
letter of credit
letter of credit, commercial
leverage
leverage, financial
liabilities, current
liability

FINANCIAL TERMS

liability, double
liability, limited
liability, unlimited
licensing
LIFO
liquid capital
liquidating dividends
liquidity
load
loan
loan, broker's time
loan, call
loan, consumption
loan, downstream
loan shark
locked-in
long
long-term financing

maker
manual, budget
margin
margin call
marginal trading
market, acceptance
Massachusetts Trust
maturity date
model balance sheet
money market
money market mutual fund
mortgage
mortgage, blanket
mortgage, chattel
mortgage, closed-in
mortgage, general
mortgage, open-end
mortgage, real estate
mutual fund

negotiable instrument
net income
net loss
net sales

net worth
nonnotification plan
nonrecourse paper
no-par stock
no protest
note
note, bank
note, promissory
notes payable
notice of dishonor
notice of protest
notification plan
N.P.

odd-lot
off the books
offer
open-end investment company
open-end investment trust
order, limit
overcapitalized
overdraw
over-the-counter
over-the-counter market
owners' equity

paper, cash
paper loss
paper profit
partial registration
payee
pecuniary interest
pledged securities
portfolio
posting
posting reference
preemptive right
preferred stock
premium
present worth
prime rate
principal
privileged subscriptions

411

FINANCIAL TERMS

proceeds
profit
profit, net
profit, operating
profit, undivided
profit and loss statement
profit margin
profit motive
profit sharing
profit taking
property tax
prospectus
provincial tax
proxy
proxy fight
public finance
puts and calls

quick assets

raiding
rate of exchange
rate of return
rate of return on investment
ratio, acid test
ratio, balance sheet
ratio, current
ratio, debt
ratio, financial
ratio, liquidity
ratio, net worth
ratio, operating
ratio, price earnings
ratio, quick
recapitalization
reconciliation of bank balance
recourse paper
redemption provision
rediscount
refunding
register, bond
registered representative

registrar
repayment
report, cost
reserve
reserve, central bank
reserves, pyramided
reserves, secondary
revenue
revenue, marginal
rights
risk capital
roll-overs

sales tax
scrip
scrip dividend
seat
SEC
Securities and Exchange Commission (SEC)
secondary distribution
secondary offering
securities
security exchange
selling short
senior security
servicing a bond
share
share warrant
shoe-string banking
short
short-term financing
sinking fund
sinking fund reserve
solvent
special situations
specialist
speculator
spin-off
spot market
spread

stabilization
stand-by underwriting
state income tax
sterilization of reserves
stock
stock, authorized
stock, blue chip
stock, capital
stock, convertible
stock, cumulative
stock, fully paid and nonassessable
stock, issued
stock, low-par-value
stock, noncumulative
stock, nonparticipating
stock, nonvoting
stock, no-par-value
stock, participating
stock, part-paid and assessable
stock, par-value
stock, treasuring
stock, voting
stock averages
stock book
stock certificate
stock dividend
stock exchange
stock option
stock power
stock purchase option
stock purchase warrant
stock split
stock transfer tax
stock warrant
stockholder
street certificates
street name
subscription agreement
subscription date
subscription warrant
surplus

surplus, appropriated
surplus, capital-reduction
surplus, paid-in

tariff
tax
tax, capital gains
tax, consumption
tax, entrance
tax, estate
tax, excise
tax, federal income
tax, franchise
tax, inheritance
tax, organization
tax, privilege
tax, proportional
tax, regressive
tax, regulatory
tax, severance
tax, transfer
tax, use
tax, withholding
tax adjustment
tax bracket
tax loss carryover
taxation
taxes, stamp
tender offer
ticker tape
tight money
time deposit
trade acceptance
trade discount
trade discount, functional
trade discount, pure
trading on the equity
trading posts
trading range
transfer agent
transfer and inheritance tax

FINANCIAL TERMS

trans-lux
treasurer
treasury stock
trial balance
trust fund
trust fund, common
trust receipt

undercapitalized
underwriter
underwriting
underwriting syndicate
unsecured loan
usury
usury laws

value, replacement
venture capital
voucher system

warrant
watered stock
wire fate items
wire transfer
working capital
working sheet
write-off

yield

zero balance account
zero base budgeting

General Terms
absentee ownership
absolute advantage
account executive
accountability
accreditation
acquisition
across-the-board
ad hoc committee
adjustment
adjustment letter

administration
administrator
advance
agate line
agent
agent, export
agent, import
air express
air freight
allowance
amalgamation
apple polisher
applicant
application
appraisal
apprenticeship
arbitration
arithmetic average
array
articles of incorporation
articles of partnership
assembling
attrition
audimeter
automation
average
average, moving

backlog
back order
bad debt
balance of stores ledger
balance of trade
balance of trade, favorable
balance of trade, unfavorable
ballpark figure
bank
bank, national
bank, savings
bank, state
bank, wildcat
bank holiday
barometers

GENERAL TERMS

barter
bath
Better Business Bureau
bid
Big Three
billing
billing, cycle
bill of lading
bill of lading, non-negotiable
bill of lading, order
bill of lading, straight
bill of material
bill of sale
bill of sale, conditional
bimodal distribution
blackbox
black market
blind advertisement
block style
board of directors
boiler room operation
bond, contract
boom
boot
bottleneck inflation
boycott
brainstorming
branch
brand
brand, national
brassage
budget, materials
budget, production
budget calendar
budget deficit
budget department
budget surplus
budget variance
building codes
built-in stabilizers
bulge
bulk station operator

bullion
bureaucracy
bureaucrat
business
business, service
business administration
business communications
business conditions
business cycle
buyer
buying, forward
buying, reciprocal
buying habits
buying power
buzzwords
by-laws
by-product

capital
capital goods
capital stock
capitalist
cargo
carrier
carrier, common
carrier, private
carrying charge
cartel
cash
cash, petty
cash disbursements
cash discount
cash journal
cash receipts
cash surrender value
cash value
chain, voluntary
chain store
Chamber of Commerce
chart
check

GENERAL TERMS

check, cashier's
check, certified
check, post-dated
check, stop-payment
check, traveler's
circular industry
claim letter
class rate
clerical work
clip-sheet
coinage
coinage, free
collection
collection letter
collection procedure
collective bargaining
collusive bargaining
combination, conglomerate
combination, corporate
combination, horizontal
combination, vertical
commerce
commercial
commercial art
committee
committee organization
commodity
commodity approach
commodity exchange
commodity rate
common carrier
common stock
communications
community of interests
company
company store
comparative advantage
competition
competition, imperfect
competition, perfect
competition, pure

competition, unfair
competitor
complimentary close
comptroller, controller
computing
concern
conference
conflict resolution
consignee
consignment
consignor
consolidation
constant
consumer
consumer finance
consumer price index (CPI)
consumption
contract carrier
contracts, tying
control
control, flow
control, inventory
control, materials
control, order
control, quantity
cooling-off period
cooperative (co-op)
cooperative, farmer's
co-owner
copy
copyright
corporate personality
corporate seal
corporation
corporation, alien
corporation, closed
corporation, domestic
corporation, foreign
corporation, nonstock
corporation, not-for-profit
corporation, open

GENERAL TERMS

corporation, private
corporation, public
corporation charter
correlation
cost
cost, fixed
cost, marginal
cost, unit
cost, variable
cost-benefit analysis
cost control, accounting
cost control, operational
cost of goods sold
cost of living
cost-plus contract
cost-plus pricing
cost-plus inflation
costs, direct
costs, historical
costs, indirect
costs, standard
counterfeit money
counter-offer
coupon
C.P.A.
CPM
credit card
credit letter
credit rating
credit report
credit transaction
credit union
creeping inflation
currency
curve
curve, deviation
custom manufacture
customer
customs duty
cycles
cyclical variation

data
date of record
debasement
debit
debt
debtor
decentralizing
decile
decision tree
decline
deductible
defalcation
deferred
deficit financing
deflation
delivery, conditional
delivery, unconditional
demand
demand, consumer
demand, elastic
demand, inelastic
demand curve
demand-pull inflation
demand schedule
demonstration
department
departmentalization
departmental operation
depletion
deposit
deposit currency
depositor
depreciation
depression
deregulation
design
design, package
deskilled
desterilization of reserves
devaluation
development credit corporation

GENERAL TERMS

deviation, average
deviation, standard
diminishing returns, law of
directive
directors
disclaimer clause
discounts, chain
dispatching
disposable income
diversification
donor
dummy director
dumping
Dun & Bradstreet, Inc.

economic order quantity
economic wealth
economics
economy
elasticity of demand
electrotypes
em
end product
enterprise
enterprise, free
enterprise, private
entrepreneur
E.O.M.
equilibrium
equipment
ethics, business
ethics, code of
evaluation
exchange
expansion
expedite
expenditure
exporter
express mail
extractive industry
extrapolation

fabricating

fair value
farmers' market
feature syndicate
fee
fee simple
FIFO
file
file, tickler
fiscal
fiscal agent
fiscal policy
fiscal year
fleet
flow diagram
flow of work
forecasting
forecasting, sales
foreign exchange
foreman
forfeit
forgery
form letter
formula investing
Fortune 500
founders' shares
fraud
free good
frequency
frequency distribution
functional approach
functional organization
fundamental analysis

gang boss
Gantt chart
GNP
going concern
gold-bricking
goldsmith's note
gold standard
goods
goods, durable
goods, economic

goods, finished
goods, free
goods, hard
goods, insistence
goods, semifinished
goods, soft
goods, unascertained
goodwill
grant
graphic art production
greenbacks
gross national product (GNP)
gypsy

half-tone reproduction
hands-on test
headhunter
hedging
histogram
holding company
hush money

impact
import quotas
importer
in kind
in transit
incentives
income
indirect labor
indoctrination
inducement
induction
industrial democracy
industrial distributor
industrial fatigue
industrial goods
industrial psychologist
industrial relations
Industrial Revolution
industry
industry, analytic

industry, assembly
industry, synthetic
inflation
input
inquiry
inserts
insistence goods
inspection
institutional approach
intaglio printing
interchange reports
interpolation
interstate commerce
interview
interview, depth
interviewing, jury system
intransitu
intrinsic reward
inventory
inventory float
inventory turnover
invoice
IRA

jewelers' block policy
job shop
joint account
joint stock company
joint tenants
joint venture
journeyman

Keogh Plan
kickback
kiting

labeling, descriptive
labeling, grade
labels
laissez-faire
landlord
layout
layout, art

GENERAL TERMS

layout, plant
lead time
leasehold
legal tender
lessee
lessor
letter of credit, traveler's
letterpress printing
licensing
LIFO
limited
limited partnership
line and staff organization
line cut
line-haul service
line organization
lines of authority
linotype
liquid assets
liquidate
lithography
live program
load ahead schedule
lot, carload
lot, less than carload
luxury trade

machine, addressograph
maintenance
maintenance, plant
management
management, absentee
management, administrative
management, centralized
management, decentralized
management, intermediate
management, middle
management, operating
management, personnel
management, sales
management audit
management by exception

management by objectives
management consultant
management control
management functions
management specialization
manager
manifest
manpower
manual, budget
manual, organization
manual, policy
manual, procedure
manufacturer's agent
manufacturers' output floater
manufacturing
marginal productivity
marginal revenue
marginal utility
margin-of-safety
mass production
master schedule
materials
materials flow
materials shortage
matrice
matrix
mats
maximil rate
MBA
MBWA
mechanization
media
median
Medicaid
Medicare
medium
medium of exchange
memorandum
mentor
mercantile
merger
methods improvement

GENERAL TERMS

microfilm
micromotion
midlife crisis
mill
milline rate
minimal rate
minutes of the meeting
miscellaneous
mobile unit
mode
Mom and Pop shop
money
money, cheap
money, coined
money, earnest
money, fiat
money, functions of
money, paper
money changer
money order
monochromatic
monopoly
monopoly power
monopoly price
monotype
montage
montage, photo
motion study
multilith
multiplier
mutual fund

near money
necessities
negligence
negotiation
nepotism
network radio
newsletter
news release
Nielsen survey
nonoperating company

note, Federal Reserve
note, United States
notes and accounts receivable

obsolescence
obsolete
office
office routine
old-age assistance
old boys' network
oligopoly
open-book account
open house
operating expenses
operating income
operating loss
operation sheets
operations research
option
organization
organization chart
output
output unit
overhead
overhead, factory
overproduction

package engineering
packaging
panel discussion
paper, bond
paper, carbon
paper, cash
paper, ledger
paper, manifold
paper, mimeo bond
paper, onion skin
paper, safety
parent company
parity
partner, junior

GENERAL TERMS

partner, senior
partner, silent
partnership
partnership, limited
partnership, mining
pass the dividend
past due account
patent
patent pool
patent release
pay, deferred
pecuniary interest
peddler car
pension
pension fund
per capita income
percent
per diem
personal property
personal property, intangible
personal property, tangible
personality
PERT
photo-offset
physical plant
pica
picture continuity
picture panel
piece rate
piggyback
pilfering
pipe lines
pits
planning section
planograph
plural-voting stock
policy, company
pool
pool, output
pool, price and profit
pool, territorial

pool car service
portfolio
precision manufactured
press agent
press conference
press kit
price, equilibrium
price, nominal
price controls
price system
primary data
principal
process
process engineer
processing unit
producer
product
product analysis
product development
production
production, continuous-process
production, factors of
production, specific-order
production, speculative
production committee
production control
production records
productive capacity
products, joint
profit
profit, net
profit, operating
profit, undivided
profit center
profit margin
Program Evaluation and Review
    Technique (PERT)
projection
promoter
promotion
proof

GENERAL TERMS

proofread
property, common
property, community
property, private
proposition
proprietorship
pro rata
prospect
prosperity
protest
proxy
proxy fight
prudent man rule
psychological need
public
public finance
public market
public opinion
public relations
public utility
publicity
pulse survey
pump-priming
purchase order
purchase record
purchase requisition
purchases, charge-take
purchasing
purchasing, centralized
purchasing, contract
purchasing, scheduled
purchasing, speculative
purchasing department
purchasing power
pyramiding

qualifications
quality control
quartile
questionnaire
quintile
quorum

quotation record
raiding
random sampling
range
rat race
rates, class
rates, commodity
rates, exception
ratio
ratio, inventory turnover
raw materials
real estate
real income
real property
realty
rebate
receiving department
recession
reconcile
record, finished stock
recover
red tape
reference
release
relief printing
reminder letter
remittance
rent
reorganization
report
report, annual
report, executive
report, progress
representative sample
reprint
requisition
requisition, purchasing
research
research, public opinion
reserve, central bank
reserves, pyramided

GENERAL TERMS

reserves, secondary
resident buyer
resume
retainer
retention
reverse discrimination
ring
role-playing
rolling stock
round table conference
route sheet
routing
rule of exceptions

sabotage
sale
salvaging
sampling
sandwich criticism
scalar chain
scale
scale, graphic
scale, linear
scalping
scarcity
scatter chart
scatter diagram
scheduling
scrip
sealed bids
seasonal variation
secondary data
secular trend
seigniorage
self-employed
seller
service, field
service, janitor
service business
service department
services
setup time

shipping
shopping center, controlled
SIC
silent partner
silk-screen printing
simo chart
single proprietorship
Social Security
sole proprietor
sole proprietorship
special event
speculator
square deal
standard
standard manufacture
standard of living
standardization
stand-by equipment
statement of account
state of the art
statistical data
statistical table
statistics
stencil
stereotypes
stock power
stockholder
stop order
stop payment
stores' credit slip
subcontractor
subscriber
subsidiary
subsistence
supplier
supply
supply curve
supply schedule
supply side economics
survey
survivors' benefits
sustaining program

GENERAL TERMS

switchboard
switching and terminal services
syndicate
syndicate, picture

tag board
tally sheet
tariff
teacher's kit
technical analysis
technique
technology
telecommunication
telephoto
teletype
teletypesetter
teller
tender
terminal services
testing
therbligs
tickler file
tight money
time series
tolerance
toll and equipment section
tooling
top executive
top management
trade association
trade journal
trademark
trade name
trade secret
trader
traffic
traffic control
traffic density
transcribed program
transit
transportation
transportation, pipeline

transposition
traveler's check
treasury currency
trend
troubleshooting
trust company
typography

under the table
unit cost

valuation
value
variable
vari-type
VCR
vending machine
vendor
vendor's record
vertical integration
vested
vested interest
vocational training
voting, cumulative
voting by proxy
voting trust
voucher

waiver of notice form
warehouse
warehouse, receipt
warehousing
warehousing, field
wasting-asset corporation
wealth
wealth, economic
wealth, private
wealth, social
weighted average
welfare
winding up
wiped out
wire service

work-in-process
work sheet
written report

"you" attitude

zero base inventory
zero defects
zip code
zip + 4
zone campaign
zoning

Insurance Terms
accidental death
act of God
actuary
adjustor
annuitant
annuity
annuity, group
annuity, joint survivorship
assessment
assigned risk
assignment, absolute
assignment, collateral
automatic premium loan

beneficiary
binder
blanket policy
bond, blanket position
bond, fidelity
bond, fiduciary
bond, forgery and alteration
bond, license and permit
bond, lost-instrument
bond, names-schedule
bond, petitioning or creditors'
bond, position-schedule

bond, public-official
bond, sheriff indemnity
broker

casualty
claim
coinsurance clause
compensatory damage
comprehensive coverage
concealment
conversion privilege

death benefits
donee beneficiary
double indemnity

endowment policy
extended term insurance

fidelity bond
floater (floating policy)

grace period

health benefits
health maintenance organization (HMO)
homeowner's policy

insolvency clause
insurable interest
insurance
insurance, accident and sickness
insurance, accidental death and dismemberment
insurance, accounts receivable
insurance, broad form personal theft
insurance, builder's risk
insurance, cargo
insurance, casualty
insurance, collision
insurance, credit
insurance, endowment
insurance, fire
insurance, freight

INSURANCE TERMS

insurance, group
insurance, hospitalization
insurance, hull
insurance, industrial
insurance, inland marine
insurance, key-man
insurance, liability
insurance, life
insurance, limited payment life
insurance, marine
insurance, mercantile open-stock burglary
insurance, ordinary life
insurance, products liability
insurance, property damage
insurance, term
insurance, unemployment
insurance, workers' compensation
insurance policy

lapse
lump sum payment

major medical insurance
maternity benefits
mortality rate
mortality table
mutual insurance company

old-age and survivors' benefits
optional modes of settlement

paid-up insurance
parcel post insurance
pension
personal property floater
premium
premium, annual
premium, monthly
product liability

reinstatement
replacement cost
risk
risk, insurable

salesmen's floater
self-insurance
stock insurance company
subrogation
suicide clause
surety bond

transportation floater

underwriter

value, replacement

waiver

Legal Terms
acceptance
accounts, uncollectible and execution proof
act of God
administrative law
affidavit
affirmative action
after-acquired clause
agency
agent
amicus curiae
antitrust
appeal
appellant
arrangement
articles of incorporation
articles of partnership
assign
assignee
assignment
assignment, absolute
attachment

bailee
bailment
bailment, gratuitous
bailment, storage

LEGAL TERMS

bailment, warehouse
Bakke decision
bankruptcy
bankruptcy, involuntary
bankruptcy, voluntary
bequest
bilateral contract
blue laws
blue sky law
bond, bail
bond, cost
bond, divisional
bond, petitioning or creditors'
breach of contract
breach of promise
bulk sales laws
business law
business trust

caveat emptor
certificate of convenience and necessity
certificate of incorporation
cestui que trust
Chapter 11
charter
civil law
Civil Rights Act
commercial law
common law
compensatory damage
composition
conditional sale
consideration
conspiracy to restrain trade
contract
contract, conditional sales
contract, illegal
conveyance
corporation
corporation, alien
corporation, closed

corporation, domestic
corporation, foreign
corporation, nonstock
corporation, not-for-profit
corporation, open
corporation, private
corporation, public
corporation charter
creditor
creditor, general
creditor, preferred
creditor beneficiary

deed
deed, quit claim
deed, warranty
default
defendant
disaffirmance
disclaimer clause
discrimination
dishonor
donee beneficiary
donor
drawee
drawer

easement
EEOC
eminent domain
employment-at-will
endorsement
endorsement, blank
endorsement, conditional
endorsement, qualified
endorsement, restrictive
endorsement, special
endorser, accomodation
equity
escape clause
escrow
estoppel

LEGAL TERMS

executor, executrix
extension agreement

fair trade
fee simple
fiduciary
fraud
frozen account

garnishment
grandfather clause
guarantee
guarantor
guaranty

holder in due course

infirmity
injunction
insolvency clause
insolvent
instrument
interlocking directorate
intestate

joint liability
judgment creditor
judgment debtor

legacy
legal entity
legal personality
lien
lien, carrier's
lien, common law
lien, mechanic's
limited

mortgage
mortgage, blanket
mortgage, chattel
mortgage, closed-in
mortgage, general
mortgage, open-end
mortgage, real estate

negotiable instrument
negotiation
nonforfeiture values

Occupational Safety and Health Administration (OSHA)

petition
plaintiff
pledge
power of attorney
presentment
product liability
property, community
prudent man rule

quit claim deed
quorum
quota system

receiver
receivership
referee
replevin
res
restraint of trade
retainer
right of survivorship
right-to-work laws

sale, forced
seal of corporation
settlor
statutory law
subrogation
summons
surety
surety bond
suretyship

tenancy
tenant
tenants in common
title

LEGAL TERMS

title, absolute
tort
trust
trust fund
trust fund, common
trustee
trusteed pension plan

ultra vires act
uniform commercial code (UCC)
unfair trade laws
usury laws

warranty
warranty, express
warranty, implied

yellow dog contract

Marketing Terms
account, open-book
account executive
advance card
advance press
advertising, black and white
advertising, color
advertising, commodity
advertising, cooperative
advertising, direct mail
advertising, institutional
advertising, point of purchase
advertising, public relations
advertising, remembrance
advertising, word of mouth
advertising agency
advertising allowance
advertising campaign
advertising folder
advertising manager
advertising media
advertising promotion
advertising specialty

aftermarket sales
agent
agent, export
agent, import
appeal
audience

bargain counter
basing point price system
blanket order
blindpair comparison
broadside
budget, advertising
budget, sales
buyer's market

C.A.F.
canned sales talk
canvassing
cash discount
caveat emptor
C.B.D.
channels of distribution
charge account
charge plan
C.I.F.
classified advertising
clincher
close, the
closed-end question
C.O.D.
cold call
combination sales
commission
commission house
commission merchant
competition
competition, imperfect
competition, perfect
competition, pure
competition, unfair
competitor

MARKETING TERMS

conditional sale
consignee
consignment
consignor
consumer
consumer, ultimate
consumer goods
consumer motivation
consumer survey
contracts, tying
control, sales
convenience goods
copy
corporate chain
cost, distribution
customer

dating
dating codes
dealer
demographic characteristics
design, package
desk-jobber
discount
discount, earned
discount, quantity
discount, time
discount, trade
discount, unearned
discount house
discounts, chain
display
display, point of sale
display, window
distribution
distribution costs
distributor
drawing account
drop-shipper
dual pricing

emporium

end product
exclusive selling agent
expense, selling

field training
financing, wholesale
financing plan, retail
fire sale
F.O.B. destination
F.O.B. shipping point
focus group
forecasting, sales
franchise
franchise fee

gatefold advertisement
gimmick

handbills

impact
impulse buying
industrial distributor
insert
installment buying
installment plan
installment selling
institutional approach
interview, depth
interview, panel

jobber
job lot
junk mail

key account

lead
lead report
list price
list selection
loss leader

mailing list
mail order
mail-order house

MARKETING TERMS

management, sales
manufacturers' representative
markdown
market
market analysis
market penetration
market position
market potential
market segmentation
market share
market value
marketing
marketing campaign
marketing functions
marketing mix
marketing plan
marketing policy
marketing research
markup
mass market
mass marketing inquiries
mass selling
merchandise
merchandise manager
merchandising
merchant
merchant middleman
middleman
middleman, agent
middleman, functional
middleman, merchant
missionary salesman
money, earnest
monopoly price
motivation research

national advertising
Nielsen survey

one-price house
open-book account
open-end question

opinion survey
outlet

package deal
packaging
P.R. stunt
price
price, actual
price, nominal
price, normal
price ceiling
price controls
price cutting
price fixing
price lines
price making
price sensitivity
price war
pricing
product identification
product life cycle
product line
promotional allowance
psychographic characteristics

qualify

rack-jobber
rate card
ratio, sales
ratio, volume-expense-calls
research, market
research, public opinion
retail
retail advertising
retail chain
retail distribution
retailer

sales on approval
sale or return
sales budget
sales contest

sales convention
sales curve
sales division
sales force
sales forecast
sales letter
sales management
sales manager
sales pitch
sales potential
sales presentation
sales program
sales promotion
sales quota
sales slip
sales talk
sales tax
sales territory
sales volume
salesmanship
salesmen's floater
saleswise
sealed bids
seasonal route
sellers' market
selling
selling, door-to-door
selling, mail order
selling, retail
selling agent
shopping goods
signature
signed advertisement
single-line store
slogan
solicit
solicited reply
space buying
special event
special-trip route
specialty goods

specialty store
split commission
sponsored program
spot announcement
spot field investigation
spot radio
stopper, advertising
store
store, independent
storing
straight commission
stuffer
stunts
survey, attitude
swing route

target market
telemarketing
terms
terms of sale
test market
testimonial
time buying
trade channel
trade discount
trade discount, functional
trade discount, pure
trademark
trade name
trade show
trading area
traffic stopper
turnover
two-price house

universe

variety store

wagon distributor
wagon jobber
warranty
warranty, express

MARKETING TERMS

warranty, implied
white space
wholesale
wholesale merchant
wholesaler
wholesaler, limited-function
wholesaler, specialty
wholesaler, voluntary-chain

zone campaign

Personnel Terms
absenteeism
across-the-board
administrative assistant
affirmative action
age certification
annuity, group
annual earnings
applicant
appraisal, performance
arbitration
arbitration, voluntary
assertiveness training
assignment of wages

back pay
Bakke decision
bargaining
bargaining, collective
bargaining, individual
base pay
benchmark jobs
benefit period
blackleg
blanket agreement
blue collar workers
bond, fidelity
bond, names-schedule
bonus
bonus, attendance
bonus, cost of living

bonus, merit
bonus, recruitment
bonus, stock
bookkeeper
boycott
boycott, primary
boycott, secondary
branch manager
burnout
buyer

cafeteria benefits
call-in-time
career counseling
CEO
CFO
chairman of the board
character reference
chief executive officer
chief financial officer
clerical work
closed shop
collective bargaining
company man
comparable worth
compensation
compensation, monetary
compensation, unemployment
conflict of interest
cooling-off period
cost-of-living increase

day care
dead end position
deadheading
deadwood
decruitment
deferred compensation
deferred wage increase
demotion
department head
deskilled

differentials (wage, skill, shift)
discharge
discrimination
double time
EAP
EEOC
emolument
employee
employee assistance program
employee relations
employee stock ownership plan
employer
employment
employment-at-will
employment agency
ergonomics
escalator clause
escape clause
ESOP
executive
executive, chief
executive, junior

fair employment practices
featherbedding
fidelity bond
fixed benefits plan
flat rate
flexitime
foreman
fringe benefits

gang boss
garnishment
get the sack
going over one's head
goldbricking
golden handcuffs
golden handshake
golden parachute
gopher
grandfather clause

grey collar worker
grievance
grievance procedure

handbook, employee
handicapped worker
hazard pay
headhunter
health benefits
hit the deck
human resources
human resources accounting
human resources management (HRM)

individual retirement account
insurance, group
insurance, hospitalization
insurance, key-man
insurance, unemployment
interview, exit
interview, preliminary
interview, selection
IRA

job, key
job analysis
job cycle
job description
job evaluation
job hopping
job security
job sharing
job specifications
journeyman

kicked upstairs

labor force
labor movement
labor organization
labor problems
labor relations
labor turnover
labor union

PERSONNEL TERMS

layoff
leave of absence
loaned servant
lockout

man hour
management
management, absentee
management, administrative
management, centralized
management, decentralized
management, intermediate
management, middle
management, operating
management, personnel
management, sales
management, sales
management functions
manual, policy
manual, procedure
maternity benefits
maternity leave
MBWA (management by walking around)
mechanical aptitude tests
mediation
merit increase
merit rating
minimum wage
moonlighting
morale, employee
motion study

National Labor Relations Board (NLRB)
negative stimulus
NLRB

occupational disease
occupational hazard
Occupational Safety and Health Administration (OSHA)
office manager

office personnel
officer
old-age and survivors' benefits
old-age assistance
open shop
operant conditioning
organization
organization chart
organized labor
OSHA
outpiacement
overtime

part shift
pay, deferred
pay, separation
payroll
payroll deductions
payroll sheets
pecking order
per diem
performance appraisal
perquisites (perks)
personnel
personnel management
picketing
piece wage
placement
placement bureau
point system
position
preferential union shop
premium pay
president
probationary period
production committee
production manager

qualify
quality circles
quit
quota system

PERSONNEL TERMS

rating, analytic
rating scale
recruitment
requisition, personnel
resignation
rest period
retirement
retirement fund
rotating internship
rotating shift

sabotage
safety program
salary
sales force
sales management
sales manager
scab
secretary
secretary of corporation
section foreman
security, employee
semiskilled workers
seniority
separation
severance
severance pay
shift
shift, day
shift, graveyard
shift, swing
shift premium plan
shop disciplinarian
shop steward
skilled workers
span of control
split commission
split shift
stabilization, salary
stabilization, wage
staff
staff assistant

staff function
standard of living
strike
strike, jurisdictional
strike benefits
structural unemployment
subordinate
subsistence allowance
suggestion box
superintendent
supervision
supervisor
supervisor, first line
sweatshop

task force
tax, withholding
team player
test, aptitude
test, intelligence
test, interest
test, performance
test, personality
test, proficiency
test, projective
test, paper and pencil
Theory X and Theory Y
Theory Z
time and motion study
timekeeping
time study
top executive
top management
trade union
traffic manager
training
training, formal
training, informal
training, on-the-job
transfer
transfer, lateral
treasurer

PERSONNEL TERMS

trusteed pension plan
turnover
type A personality

unemployment
unemployment, chronic
unemployment, cyclical
unemployment, frictional
unemployment, seasonal
unemployment, technological
unemployment, voluntary
unemployment compensation
union
union, company
union, craft
union, industrial
union, trade
union recognition
union shop
union steward
unskilled workers

vacation
vestibule training
vice president

wage
wage, average
wage, guaranteed annual
wage, money
wage, real
wage, time
wage incentive
wages, indirect
walkout
welfare fund
whistleblower
workaholic
work hours
work stoppage
working conditions

yellow dog contract